CARD PLAY MADE EASY 3:
Trump Management

Most of the contracts that you play are suit contracts. The presence of a trump suit provides more choices and also more dangers. If you find yourself failing in a trump contract which you see afterwards that you could and should have made, all that is necessary is to acquire the skill to be wise before the event instead of after. Forget the contracts which you cannot make but do something about those which can succeed. What you want is a pat on the back for congratulations, not for sympathy.

The *CARD PLAY MADE EASY* series aims to impart skills which are not too difficult to recognise and to put into practice. The third book in our series deals solely with trump contracts. The topics include how to create more winners and how to eliminate losers, how to spot the defenders' plans and how to thwart them and how to choose the best line when you have a number of options. After studying the advice and deals in these pages, you are bound to become a more successful declarer.

CARD PLAY MADE EASY 3:

TRUMP MANAGEMENT

Ron Klinger & Andrew Kambites

LONDON

VICTOR GOLLANCZ

in association with

PETER CRAWLEY

First published in Great Britain 1998
in association with Peter Crawley
by Victor Gollancz
An imprint of the Cassell Group
Wellington House, 125 Strand, London WC2R 0BB

A catalogue record for this book
is available from the British Library

ISBN 0 575 06596 6

Typeset in Australia by Modern Bridge Publications,
60 Kameruka Road, Northbridge, NSW 2063, Australia

Printed in Great Britain by
St Edmundsbury Press Ltd, Bury St Edmunds, Suffolk

CONTENTS

INTRODUCTION

When we first learn to play, one of the first pieces of advice we receive are, 'Draw trumps as soon as possible'. A colourful teacher might even refer to the tramps along the River Thames who are there only because they failed to draw trumps soon enough. Alas, when we put this tip into practice, we find that this is not the longed for recipe for success. On many occasions playing trumps early and often can spell defeat. A good teacher will continue the allusion by referring to the tramps in Hyde Park: 'They are the ones who drew trumps too soon.'

Tramps and trumps do not have to go together. What is needed is the understanding when it is better not to play trumps at once and that is precisely what this book sets out to do. Each chapter covers a different area of trump play and illustrates the required skill with plentiful examples.

Some learning applicable to trump contracts has appeared in the previous books in this series, safety plays and endplays in Book 1 and fundamental card combinations in Book 2. As far as possible, the topics in this book avoid areas previously covered, but themes can be inextricably interwoven and knowledge from the earlier books can be relevant and useful to the task at hand.

Chapters 1-7 end with a collection of declarer problems on the relevant area and the recommended line of play for each. After the final chapter there is a very lengthy quiz on all aspects of the book. It is important to strive to answer each of the questions yourself before consulting the solution. A serious effort here will translate into better performance at the table where no one provides you with a solution to which you can conveniently refer.

Your aim in all the problems is to make your contract. Overtricks or undertricks are of no concern.

Ron Klinger and Andrew Kambites

Chapter 1

WINNERS AND LOSERS

In about 60% of all suit contracts, declarer sets about drawing the enemy trumps upon gaining the lead for the first time. In most of the deals in this book, that will not happen.

The reason is simple. A declarer who has plenty of winners and not too many losers rushes to draw trumps before falling victim to an unwelcome enemy ruff. Such hands are easy to play. It is when declarer is short of tricks that this precaution may become a luxury you cannot afford. Such hands require greater skill and are naturally of more interest.

Consider the following deal:

You	*Dummy*
♠ A K 6 4 3	♠ 9 8 7 2
♡ A K	♡ 7 5 2
◇ K Q	◇ 9 6 5 3
♣ A 5 3 2	♣ J 4

Contract : 4♠. Lead: ♡Q.

It is easy enough to count eleven tricks including two club ruffs if trumps break 2-2 but it could be fatal to start by drawing two rounds of trumps. Suppose you win with the ♡A, cash ♠A, ♠K and find that the trumps are 3-1. You have to concede a club before you can ruff two clubs in dummy. This may enable the defender with the master trump to gain the lead and draw two of your trumps. You will then be unable to ruff two clubs with only one trump in dummy.

You need to concede the club loser earlier. Correct technique is to cash only the ♠A at trick 2 and then play a low club from both hands. When you regain the lead, you can cash the ♠K before embarking on the club ruffs.

♠ A K Q 7 4 3	**N**	♠ 6 5
♡ A K	**W E**	♡ 7 6 4
◇ A 3 2	**S**	◇ 10 5 4
♣ A 4		♣ K Q J 10 3

Contract : 6♠. Lead: ♡Q.

If spades are 3-2, the only problem will be to avoid any acrimony in discussing how you missed 7NT. The hand becomes interesting only after you win the lead, cash the A-K of spades and an opponent shows out on the second round. How would you continue?

On many hands it would be correct to cash the ♠Q and then abandon trumps, allowing the opponent with the master trump to score it at will. 'If there is one trump out and it is better than yours, leave it out,' is good advice most of the time.

An exception arises when dummy has a long, strong suit and no outside entry. On this deal, cash the ♠Q and play a fourth spade. Then the slam cannot be defeated. If you cash ♠A, ♠K, ♠Q, leave the last trump out and start on clubs, an enemy ruff on the second or third club will beat you. Make the most of your good fortune in escaping a diamond lead by giving the defence their trump trick before you start on the clubs.

♠ K Q J 10 5	**N**	♠ 9 8 7 4
♡ 7 5 3	**W E**	♡ K
◇ Q 3	**S**	◇ K J 10 7 4
♣ A 8 7		♣ K 5 2

Contract : 4♠. Lead: ♣Q.

The club lead threatens you with a loser in each suit. As you have to lose to the missing aces, you must give top priority to eliminating the club loser. The only way is to discard a club on dummy's diamonds. There is no time to start on trumps. Win with the ♣A (retaining the ♣K as an entry to dummy) and lead the ◇Q. You will probably fail unless diamonds are 3-3 but that is your only chance.

On the previous deal, you had plenty of winners but needed to appreciate the danger of too many losers. There is a similar theme here:

♠ A 4 3		♠ K Q J 9
♡ Q 10 9 6 4	N	♡ K J 7 3
◇ A J 3	W E	◇ 7 6 2
♣ 7 4	S	♣ A Q

Contract : 4♡. Lead: ♣2.

It is oh, so tempting to take the club finesse which will give you eleven tricks if it works. The danger is that a losing club finesse will be followed by the natural switch to diamonds. Unable to draw trumps, you will not benefit in time from the extra spade winner in dummy and are likely to lose four tricks.

To ensure your contract, as far as that is possible, take the ♣A and drive out the ♡A while you still have the diamonds under control. Later you draw trumps and discard a diamond on the fourth spade.

Another problem you might face is how to reach winners in a dummy bereft of entries except in the trump suit. Witness:

♠ A K 8 6 3 2		♠ Q 5 4
♡ K 2	N	♡ Q 7
◇ A 5	W E	◇ 8 4 3 2
♣ A K Q	S	♣ J 8 7 3

Contract : 6♠. Lead: ◇K.

No doubt partner would not have bid so much without the ♣J. Your job is to make the most of dummy's meagre assets. Take the ◇A and cash the ♠A, ♠K. Abandon trumps for the moment even if there is still one out. Cash the ♣A, ♣K, ♣Q, praying that none of these is ruffed. Then enter dummy via a spade to the queen and discard your diamond loser on the ♣J. If an opponent does ruff an early round of clubs, the slam was doomed anyway.

♠ 7 5 2   ♠ 8 6 4
♡ K Q J 10 9   ♡ A 5 2
◇ A 7   ◇ K Q 4 3 2
♣ A 8 6   ♣ 7 4

Contract : 4♡. *Leads:* ♠A, ♠K, ♠Q, followed by the ♣J.

A simple enough plan is to take the ♣A, draw trumps and then play on diamonds. If diamonds are 3-3, you are home. As the 3-3 split is well below a 50-50 chance, you should try for a better line.

Take the ♣A and start by cashing the ♡K. If trumps are 5-0, draw trumps and pray diamonds are 3-3. If all follow to the ♡K, cash ♡Q. If trumps are 4-1, draw trumps and go for the 3-3 diamond break.

If both opponents follow to two rounds of trumps, you can cater for a 4-2 split in diamonds. Leave the last trump out for the moment. Cash the ◇A, play a diamond to dummy's king and continue with a low diamond which you ruff. You discard two clubs on dummy's last two diamonds which are winners. You can reach them with a heart to dummy's ace, simultaneously drawing the last trump.

The urgent need to eliminate losers may override the technically best way to play the trump suit. Consider this:

♠ J 10 9 5 4 2   ♠ A Q 7 3
♡ A 8 5   ♡ 7 6 2
◇ A   ◇ K 7 2
♣ K Q J   ♣ 8 4 3

Contract : 4♠. *Lead:* ♡K.

Those who have read *Card Play Made Easy #2** know that to finesse is clearly the best play with this spade combination. That is not the best move here. Take the ♡A, unblock the ◇A, lead the ♠J (to tempt North to cover with the king) but rise with dummy's ace regardless and discard a heart on the ◇K.

*If not, you can improve your declarer technique by doing so soon.

```
♠ K 10 6          N          ♠ A J 2
♡ K J 10 8 6                 ♡ 9 7 5 4 3 2
♢ 9 2        W       E       ♢ A 6
♣ K Q J          S          ♣ 7 4
```

Contract : 4♡. Lead: ♠3.

The lead has been helpful but you still need to exercise great care. When this deal arose in real life, declarer lazily played the two of spades from dummy and that was enough to sink the contract.

South defended well by playing the queen of spades and West won with the king. When declarer continued with the king of clubs, South did well again by withholding the ace.

The queen of clubs came next and was won by South who switched to a diamond. With no quick entry to hand, declarer could not reach the jack of clubs to dispose of the diamond loser. When it turned out that North had both the ace and queen of hearts, the heart game was consigned to perdition.

Can you see how declarer could have succeeded?

As happens so often, the fault lay in playing too quickly to trick 1. The best move is to play the jack of spades from dummy on the opening lead. If South plays the queen, West's ten of spades becomes an entry to the West hand, while if the jack of spades wins, declarer has the king of spades as an entry. Either way declarer will be able to reach the club winner later and so discard dummy's losing diamond. Easy enough once you think of it but it is vital to see the winning move one second before you play from dummy rather than one second after.

QUIZ 1

(1) *You*   *Dummy*

    ♠ K Q J 9 8 6 5   ♠ 10 2
    ♡ J 2   ♡ A Q 7
    ◊ 9 4   ◊ A 6 3 2
    ♣ 6 4   ♣ A 8 5 3

Contract : 4♠. Lead: ◊K. Plan the play.

(2) ♠ A Q 3   ♠ K J 10 5 4

    ♡ K Q 7 4 2   ♡ J 10 9 6 3
    ◊ A Q 5   ◊ 8
    ♣ A 7   ♣ 9 6

Contract : 6♡. Lead: ♣K. Plan the play.

(3) ♠ A K 7 4 2   ♠ 8 6 5 3

    ♡ J 5   ♡ 8 6 4 3 2
    ◊ A K Q 7   ◊ 8
    ♣ A 7   ♣ 9 5 3

Contract : 4♠. Lead: ♣K. Plan the play. If this fails, will you blame partner for providing such a worthless dummy?

(4) ♠ A K Q J 9 8 7   ♠ 10
    ♡ 7 6 5   ♡ A K 9
    ◊ - - -   ◊ 8 7 5 4 3 2
    ♣ 8 4 2   ♣ A K 3

Contract : 6♠. Lead: ◊A. Eleven tricks are easy enough but where is the twelfth? Will you be able to manage if it turns out that the diamonds are 5-2?

[14]

(5) *You*   *Dummy*

    ♠ A Q 5 4 3 2   ♠ K 10 9 8

    ♡ 8 6 3   ♡ 9

    ◊ 6   ◊ 9 5 4 3 2

    ♣ A K 4   ♣ 7 6 2

Dealer North : Both vulnerable

WEST	NORTH	EAST	SOUTH
	1NT	No	4♡
4♠	No	No	5♡
No	No	5♠	No
No	Double	All pass	

Lead : ♡Q, winning, followed by the ♣Q. Plan the play.

(6) ♠ K J 9 8 7   ♠ A Q 10

    ♡ A 6   ♡ 7 4

    ◊ J 8 3 2   ◊ A K 6 4

    ♣ 7 2   ♣ A K Q J

Contract : 7♠. *Lead:* ♡Q. Plan the play to make this pushy contract.

(7) ♠ A K 9 6 5 3   ♠ 8 4 2

    ♡ 9 5   ♡ A 7 4

    ◊ A 2   ◊ 9 3

    ♣ K 6 4   ♣ A J 8 5 2

Contract : 4♠. *Lead:* ◊K. Plan the play.

(8) ♠ J 10 9 7 4 2   ♠ Q 8 6 3

    ♡ 9 4   ♡ K Q J

    ◊ J 6   ◊ A 2

    ♣ A Q J   ♣ K 7 4 3

Contract : 4♠. *Lead:* ◊K. Good luck after this unlucky lead.

(1) You have a potential loser in each suit. Suppose you take the ace of diamonds and lead a spade. They win, cash one diamond and shift to clubs. Now if the heart finesse loses, they can put you down.

The heart finesse is an optical illusion: if it wins you make two tricks in hearts and if it loses you have two tricks in hearts. Conclusion: taking the finesse does not gain a trick. Abandon the heart finesse. Take the ◊A and lead the ♡7 to your jack. If this loses, you plan to discard your club loser on the third heart.

(2) Without the club lead, you would have had ample time to draw trumps and use dummy's spades to discard the club loser. Now, to give yourself the best chance of success, you must risk two off. Take the ♣A, enter dummy with a spade and lead a diamond to your queen. If that works, dummy's club loser can be discarded on the ace of diamonds. Now you can turn your attention to the trumps.

(3) You are prepared to lose a trump trick provided that you can ruff a club and a diamond in dummy. Take the ♣A, draw one round of trumps with the ♠A, then cash the ace, king and queen of diamonds, discarding two clubs from dummy. Ruff the ♣7, return to hand with a spade to the king and ruff the ◊7.

If you start by drawing two rounds of trumps, you have no quick entry to your hand after the first ruff in dummy. Now if trumps are 3-1, the defender with the third trump may gain the lead and remove a vital ruff by drawing a third round of trumps.

(4) You must aim to establish at least one trick in diamonds. Ruff the ◊A, enter dummy with the ♠10 and ruff the ◊3. Now draw trumps. If they break 3-2, you can afford diamonds to be 5-2.

Cross to dummy with a heart and ruff a diamond. If they are 5-2, cross to dummy in clubs, play a diamond and discard a loser. Dummy still has two entries, enough to allow you to ruff a fifth diamond and still reach dummy for your established winner in diamonds, your twelfth trick.

(5) You can ruff two hearts in dummy and settle for one down or you can risk going two down to give yourself the best chance of making your doubled game. Take the ♣A at trick 2 and concede a diamond. Your prayer is that diamonds are 4-3 and trumps 2-1 with North having the ♠J. If they continue clubs, take the ♣K, finesse the ♠10, ruff a diamond, draw the last trump with the ♠K, ruff a diamond in hand, a heart in dummy and a diamond in hand. If diamonds are 4-3, dummy's last diamond is a winner. Ruff your last heart in dummy and discard the club loser on the winning diamond.

(6) There are twelve tricks on top and a singleton or doubleton ◊Q will light up your life. For an additional chance, take the ♡A, draw just two rounds of trumps and cash ◊A, ◊K. If the ◊Q is the only diamond out, play off four club winners, discarding two diamonds. If a club is ruffed, you were always going to fail. If the clubs survive (the player with the last trump has four or more clubs), ruff a diamond, play a trump to dummy, drawing their last trump, and cash your diamond winner to discard your losing heart.

(7) Take the ◊A and cash ♠A, ♠K. If trumps are 2-2, life is easy. If there is still a trump out, the best chance for ten tricks is a 3-2 break in clubs. Cash the ♣K and follow with a club to the ace, spurning the finesse, or if South has the last trump, play a club to the ace and a club back to the king. Now concede a club if the ♣Q has not dropped. On winning the ♡A, discard your heart loser on a club winner.

Do you see the danger of taking the club finesse? If this loses, South can cash a diamond and shift to hearts. You win with dummy's ace but if the ace of clubs is ruffed, the defence comes to a heart trick before you can discard your heart loser.

(8) Despite the four very obvious losers there is still a legitimate chance. Take the ◊A and cash the ♣A and ♣Q. Then overtake the ♣J with the ♣K. If clubs are 3-3, throw your diamond loser on the thirteenth club. Someone will ruff but if their trumps are A-5 and bare K, or K-5 and singleton A, no matter which opponent ruffs, the defenders will subsequently score only one trump trick.

Chapter 2

MAKING YOUR TRUMPS SEPARATELY

Players new to the game love trumping losers. Often they happily trump losers in their own hand with trumps that were going to take tricks anyway. The net effect of this may be to lose control of the trump suit. Generally speaking if you ruff in the hand with *fewer* trumps, you are generating extra tricks. You should ruff losers in the hand with *more* trumps only if you have a specific purpose in mind.

```
     ♠ A 6 5 3 2                    ♠ K 8
     ♡ 8 5 2           N            ♡ A 9 6 3
     ◊ 2           W       E        ◊ A J 4 3
     ♣ A 6 5 2         S            ♣ 7 4 3
```

Contract : 2♠. Lead: ◊K.

You have five winners on top. It is hard to see how to generate three extra tricks without utilising your low trumps by ruffing. Take the ace of diamonds and ruff a diamond, cash the ♣A and ♠A, enter dummy with the ♠K and ruff another diamond. Finally a heart to the ace allows a third diamond ruff. If diamonds have split 4-4, you have taken the first eight tricks. Let them haggle over the last five.

```
     ♠ Q J 10 8 7 2                 ♠ A K 9
     ♡ K 8 6           N            ♡ 5 2
     ◊ A 2         W       E        ◊ 7 5 4 3
     ♣ A Q            S             ♣ 8 6 4 2
```

Contract : 4♠. Lead: ♣J.

After that lead, your game is secure as long as you are not greedy! Six spades and three minor suit winners make nine tricks. To avoid three heart losers, play a heart from your hand at trick 2. If you continue hearts at every opportunity, the defenders cannot prevent you from ruffing a heart in dummy for your tenth trick.

[18]

Do you see the trap on the preceding deal? If you cross to dummy in trumps in order to play a heart to the king, you could be defeated. If North has the ace of hearts and three trumps, North could lead a trump on capturing your ♡K with the ace, and another trump from North will knock out dummy's last trump and deny you the heart ruff. That leaves you with three hearts and a diamond to lose.

Sometimes taking your ruffs in dummy can require delicate timing. How would you play 6♠ on this layout on the lead of the ♣A?

♠ A K Q 8 7 6	N	♠ J 9
♡ A K Q		♡ 5 4 3
◊ A K 6 3	W E	◊ 7 4
♣ - - -	S	♣ J 9 7 5 4 2

Without a trump lead, 7♠ has excellent chances: cash ◊A, ◊K, ruff a diamond with the ♠9, another with the ♠J and hope that they cannot score a trump trick. That does not mean you should relax and take the same line in 6♠. If you do and the ♠9 is over-ruffed by South who returns a trump, you will be facing an unsympathetic partner.

In 6♠, cash ◊A, ◊K, ruff a diamond with ♠J, return to hand and ruff a diamond with ♠9. If over-ruffed, that should be your only loser.

♠ A 7 3	N	♠ 8 4 2
♡ A K Q J 8 3		♡ 10 9 6
◊ A K Q J	W E	◊ 5 4 2
♣ - - -	S	♣ J 7 4 3

Contract : 6♡. Lead: ♣A.

6♡ is easy if trumps are 2-2 but you might still succeed if trumps are 3-1 provided that the defender with three trumps also has four or more diamonds. Ruff the ace of clubs, cash just one trump and then concede a spade. Suppose they continue spades. Take the ♠A, cash a second trump, followed by four rounds of diamonds, discarding dummy's last spade. A spade ruff in dummy is your twelfth trick.

Sometimes ruffing a side suit enables you to establish length winners but care is needed if you are to land the next two slams.

♠ 7		♠ A 5 4
♡ Q J 10 9	N	♡ A K 8 7
◊ A K 8 5 4 3	W E	◊ 7 2
♣ 6 2	S	♣ A K 7 5

Contract : 6♡. Lead: ♡2.

You may regret missing 7♡ but the task at hand is to make 6♡. If the red suits are 3-2, you will have an easy time but can you cope with a 4-1 break in both red suits?

Win the ♡A and lead a diamond to the ace. Now duck a diamond. Suppose a second trump is led. Win this in hand, lead a low diamond and ruff with the ♡K, draw trumps and run the diamonds.

If you start by playing off the ◊A, ◊K, you will be in trouble if the ◊K is ruffed and a second trump is led, if trumps are 4-1. You will be unable to ruff two diamonds in dummy and draw trumps as well.

♠ - - -		♠ A 8 4 3 2
♡ A Q J 9 8 7	N	♡ K 10 3
◊ A K 7 6 3	W E	◊ 5 4 2
♣ K 7	S	♣ A 6

Contract : 6♡. Lead: ♠K.

If hearts are 3-1 and diamonds 4-1, you are left with two diamond losers if you draw trumps. On the other hand, if you fail to draw trumps and cash ◊A, ◊K, an opponent may ruff the second diamond. Win the ♠A, play a diamond to the ace, cash ♡A and lead a heart to the ten. Lead the next diamond from dummy, catering for three trumps and a singleton diamond with South. If South ruffs the diamond, the rest is easy. If South discards, take the ◊K, give North a diamond and later ruff a diamond with dummy's last trump.

The popular way to make your trumps separately is the cross-ruff:

♠ Q J 8 7
♥ A 8 5 4
◇ A 7 4 3
♣ 2

♠ A K 10 9
♥ K 6 3 2
◇ 9
♣ A Q 7 3

Contract : 4♠. Lead: ♠2.

When cross-ruffing it is right to cash your side suit winners first, otherwise defenders can discard their losers and ruff your winners later. You might survive but it would be risky to proceed by cashing the minor suit aces and cross-ruffing the minors. If an opponent, short in a minor, discards hearts, you may find yourself unable to score any heart tricks later.

It is always sensible to start by counting your tricks, lest you err on the side of greed. You have won the first trick and six more tricks are available via the cross-ruff. You need only three tricks from the side suits. Cash your aces in hearts, diamonds and clubs and cross-ruff merrily from there. Again, you may survive but it is an unnecessary risk to try to cash a second heart. If a defender ruffs the ♥K and leads a second trump, you may well be one trick short.

♠ A Q 7 6 5
♥ A 8 4 3 2
◇ 4
♣ A K

♠ K J 9 8
♥ 9
◇ A 7 5 3 2
♣ 7 6 3

Contract : 6♠. Lead: ♣Q.

Here you need to judge when to start ruffing high to avoid a possible over-ruff followed by a trump continuation, leaving you with only eleven tricks. Cash the ♣A, ♣K, ♥A, ◇A and ruff a diamond, a heart and a diamond with low trumps. Now to be safe, cross-ruff with your trump honours, leaving you with ♠7 in hand and ♠9 in dummy. One further ruff ensures the slam.

QUIZ 2

(1)   *You*   *Dummy*

♠ A K 6 2   ♠ 7 4

♡ A K Q J 9 8 7 5   N   ♡ 10 3

                                     W   E

♢ A   ♢ 8 6 3 2

                                            S

♣ - - -   ♣ 8 6 5 3 2

Dealer East : Both vulnerable

WEST	NORTH	EAST	SOUTH
		No	1♠
6♡	No	No	No

North leads the nine of spades, on which South plays the ten. Will you be able to match your intrepid bidding with flawless play?

(2)   ♠ K Q J 10 9   N   ♠ 8 7 2

♡ K 7 4   ♡ 9

                                     W   E

♢ A K Q   ♢ 8 6 5

                                            S

♣ A K   ♣ 9 8 5 4 3 2

Contract : 4♠. Lead: ♠A, *then* ♠3. *South follows. Plan the play.*

(3)   ♠ A K Q J 10 9   N   ♠ 8 7

♡ A   ♡ K 6 4 3 2

                                     W   E

♢ A Q 5 4   ♢ J 2

                                            S

♣ A K   ♣ 7 4 3 2

Contract : 6♠. Lead: ♠2. *Plan the play.*

(4)   ♠ A Q J 10   N   ♠ K 9 8 4

♡ A 8 4 3   ♡ 9

                                     W   E

♢ 4 2   ♢ A K 7 5

                                            S

♣ 7 4 3   ♣ Q 8 6 5

Contract : 4♠. Lead: ♠2. *Plan the play.*

(5) *You*   *Dummy*

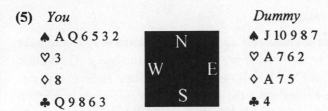

   ♠ A Q 6 5 3 2   ♠ J 10 9 8 7

   ♡ 3   ♡ A 7 6 2

   ◇ 8   ◇ A 7 5

   ♣ Q 9 8 6 3   ♣ 4

Dealer East : North-South vulnerable

WEST	NORTH	EAST	SOUTH
		No	No
1♠	Double	4♠	5◇
5♠	Double	All pass	

Lead : ◇ K. As a heart lead would defeat 5◇, you need to make 5♠ to avoid the slings and arrows of outrageous rebuke. Plan the play.

(6) ♠ A K 7 6 3   ♠ 8 4 2

    ♡ 7 5 3   ♡ A K 8

    ◇ A K 9 3   ◇ 7 4 2

    ♣ A   ♣ 9 6 5 2

Contract : 4♠. *Lead:* ♣K. Plan the play.

(7) ♠ A 7 5 2   ♠ 9 6 4 3

    ♡ 8 7 5 3   ♡ A K 6

    ◇ 2   ◇ A K 6 3

    ♣ A 6 3 2   ♣ K 8

Contract : 4♠. *Lead:* ♠K. How do you manage these meagre trumps?

(8) ♠ A K J 10 4   ♠ 7 5 3

    ♡ K Q J   ♡ A

    ◇ A 8 7   ◇ 6 5 2

    ♣ A 3   ♣ K Q J 5 4 2

Contract : 6♠. *Lead:* ◇K. What is your safest line of play?

(1) You need a spade ruff in dummy but North may easily have started with a singleton spade. If you win with the ♠A, continue with the ♠K and North ruffs, you will fail if North shifts to a trump. The solution is easy: take the ♠A and play a low spade at trick 2. You can win a trump switch in hand, ruff your other low spade, return to hand by ruffing a club and draw trumps.

(2) Without the trump lead and continuation, a heart ruff in dummy would have been easy. If you play a low heart now, the defender with the last trump might win and draw dummy's last trump. Exit heart ruff and almost certainly goodbye contract.

At trick 3 lead the ♡K. If the defender with the ♡A does not have the last trump, you will be able to ruff a heart in dummy after all.

(3) Despite the annoying trump lead, you will succeed if you can reach the ♡K. To cash the ♡A and lead a low diamond next gives you a 50% chance. If North has the ◊K, you will be all right.

There is a better line which is not only a sure thing (almost) but also elegant. Take the ♠A, unblock the ♡A and play the ◊Q. Suppose the ◊K is with South. What can South do?

If the ◊Q is allowed to win, cash the ◊A next, ruff a diamond and discard your last diamond on the ♡K to make an overtrick. If South takes the ◊Q with the ◊K, the ◊J is your entry to dummy to the ♡K.

(4) You have ten tricks on a cross-ruff as long as you start with a heart ruff first. A reasonable sequence: win ♠A, cash ◊A, ◊K, ♡A and cross-ruff the next five tricks. You still have a trump winner in hand as your tenth trick.

Suppose you start with ♠A, ♡A, ◊A, ◊K and a diamond ruff. After a heart ruff, another diamond ruff, heart ruff, you have no outside entry to your hand to score the third heart ruff. When you play a club, they can win and lead a trump to hold you to nine tricks.

(5) No rebuke for you provided that you duck a club at trick two to set up your cross-ruff. Do not cash ♠A first in case either opponent has ♠ K-4. You cannot afford to have a second round of trumps drawn.

(6) You need trumps to be 3-2 and a diamond ruff in dummy, unless diamonds are 3-3. You can stand a winner being ruffed by the defender with three trumps but it would be fatal if the hand with the doubleton trump ruffs a diamond winner or over-ruffs dummy.

This is the best sequence: Win ♣A, cash ♠A and duck a diamond. Win the next trick, cash the ♠K and the ◊A, ◊K, ruff a diamond. If you were to start with two rounds of trumps before giving up the diamond trick, you give the player with the master trump the chance to draw a third round of trumps, depriving you of the ruff in dummy.

(7) You should be all right if trumps are 3-2. As in problem (6), you must avoid the player with the doubleton trump interrupting your cross-ruff or the one with three trumps drawing a third round. To keep control, duck the ♠K. Later you draw two more trumps with the ♠A and start on your cross-ruff in the minors.

You would adopt a similar line on, say a diamond lead. Take the ace of diamonds and play a low trump from both hands. Win any return, cash the ace of spades and then switch to the cross-ruff.

(8) This will not be tough unless North began with ♠ Q-x-x-x. Take the ◊A, unblock the ♡A, come to hand with a spade to the ace and discard dummy's diamonds on your heart winners. Next play the ♠J.

If they take ♠Q, dummy can ruff a diamond exit. Come to hand with a club to the ace, draw trumps and enjoy dummy's clubs.

If the ♠J holds the trick, ruff a diamond, come to hand with ♣A, cash the ♠K and revert to clubs. You will now make your slam unless North started with a singleton club.

If North started with a doubleton club and ♠ Q-x-x-x, any attempt to ruff two diamonds in dummy will give you problems in returning to hand and will result in a trump promotion for North.

Chapter 3

A MATTER OF CHOICE

Understanding card play techniques is only the first half of the journey to bridge expertise. You also need the judgement when to employ which technique. On the deals in this chapter, you have a choice of plays. Only by counting the tricks each line will produce, considering the entry position and knowing your suit combinations (from *Card Play Made Easy 2*) will you be able to decide between their merits.

On each of these deals, you are in 4♠ and have to choose between ruffing diamonds in dummy and aiming to set up dummy's hearts.

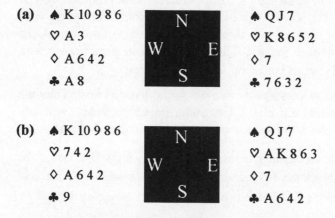

(a)
♠ K 10 9 8 6   ♠ Q J 7
♡ A 3   ♡ K 8 6 5 2
♢ A 6 4 2   ♢ 7
♣ A 8   ♣ 7 6 3 2

(b)
♠ K 10 9 8 6   ♠ Q J 7
♡ 7 4 2   ♡ A K 8 6 3
♢ A 6 4 2   ♢ 7
♣ 9   ♣ A 6 4 2

In each case North leads a spade. South takes the ace and returns a spade to which North follows. How should you continue?

In (a) ruffing diamonds in dummy would have almost guaranteed success were it not for that pesky trump lead. Now dummy has only one trump left and ruffing one diamond will yield but nine tricks. You must hope that the hearts are 3-3. Cash the ace and king of hearts and ruff a heart. If all has gone well, enter dummy (and draw the last trump) with a spade to the queen to cash two heart winners.

In (b), again you can ruff only one diamond. If you then give up a trick in hearts, they can cash two diamonds. The best chance is to duck a heart at trick 3. If the defenders persevere with a third round of trumps, all will be well if the missing hearts were 3-2 originally.

♠ K J 10 8 7 4 3
♡ A Q 5
◇ K 8 3
♣ - - -

♠ A 2
♡ K J 6 3 2
◇ 9 6 4
♣ J 8 3

Contract : 4♠. Lead: ♣A.

Taking the spade suit in isolation, the best chance to avoid a trump loser is to cash the ace and king. In the context of the whole hand, this is not the way to ensure the contract. You are safe unless South can play diamonds through your king and so you should cash the ♠A and finesse the jack. Losing to North's doubleton ♠Q will not hurt you as you can discard at least one of your diamonds on the hearts.

It would be unlucky to fail by playing ♠A and ♠K. South would have to hold ♠Q-x-x and fewer than three hearts with North holding ◇A-x-x or longer. Though this might amount to no more than 5%, why take any risk when ♠A and a spade to the jack is 100% safe?

♠ A K 10 9 6 4
♡ K 8
◇ 7 4
♣ A K 8

♠ 7 5 3
♡ A Q 2
◇ K Q J 2
♣ Q 6 3

Contract : 6♠. Lead: ♣J. When you cash ♠A, North drops the ♠J.

You must guess whether North began with ♠J singleton or ♠Q-J doubleton. It might seem the toss of a coin but there is a clue. With ♠Q-J doubleton, North might have chosen the ♠Q instead of the ♠J. In such situations it is better to assume North had no choice, that the honour was singleton. This is known as the *Principle of Restricted Choice*. Cross to dummy with a heart and finesse the ♠10.

It can pay to take into account the mental processes of the defenders.

```
♠ 8 5                    N              ♠ J 7 3 2
♡ A K 8 7 5 4                           ♡ 10 9 6
                    W         E
◊ K Q J                                 ◊ 9 7
♣ 6 2                    S              ♣ A K Q J
```

Dealer East : Both vulnerable

WEST	NORTH	EAST	SOUTH
		No	1♠
2♡	No	3♡	No
4♡	No	No	No

North leads the nine of spades, South winning with the ten. When South cashes the ♠A, North plays the ♠4. South shifts to the two of hearts. What do you make of that? How do you play?

As North began with ♠9-4 doubleton, a third spade would promote a trump trick for the defenders if North had ♡J, ♡J-x, ♡Q or ♡Q-x.

Rather than breathe a sigh of relief and pounce with a top heart, try to discover South's motive. Has South shown generosity to the point of incompetence? Could it be the fear that you might ruff low, hold the trick and expose the fact that South started with ♡Q-J-2? If you believe so, you should play a low heart now.

```
♠ A J 10 9 5 3           N              ♠ K 2
♡ 8 5                                   ♡ 9 6
                    W         E
◊ A K 8                                 ◊ 7 6 2
♣ A K                    S              ♣ 9 8 5 4 3 2
```

Contract : 4♠. Lead: ♣J.

When this deal arose, declarer decided to enlist the help of the opponents. At trick 2 West played a heart as though angling for a heart ruff in dummy. South fell for the bait by switching to a trump and thus solving declarer's real problem.

QUIZ 3

(1) *You*   *Dummy*

♠ 6 5 3 2   ♠ A 8 4

♡ K 9 8 4 2      ♡ J 10 7 3

◊ A   ◊ K Q 2

♣ A K Q   ♣ J 4 3

Dealer West : Neither side vulnerable

WEST	NORTH	EAST	SOUTH
1♡	1♠	3♡	No
4♡	No	No	No

Lead : ♠K. The ♠A wins (phew!), South playing ♠7. Plan the play.

(2) ♠ A K 9 6 4 3   ♠ J 7 5 2

♡ 6 2   ♡ A K 4

◊ K J   ◊ Q 10 5

♣ A K 3   ♣ 9 8 5

Contract : 6♠. *Lead:* ♣2, South playing the jack. Plan the play.

(3) ♠ K 6 2   ♠ 7 4 3

♡ A K 7 6 5   ♡ J 10 9 3

◊ A K Q   ◊ J 10 9 6

♣ 5 3   ♣ A K

Contract : 4♡. *Lead:* ♣J. What is your best route?

(4) ♠ Q 5   ♠ J 4 2

♡ A K   ♡ 9 6 3

◊ A K Q   ◊ 8 5 3

♣ A Q 7 5 3 2   ♣ J 8 6 4

Contract : 5♣. *Lead:* ♠A, followed by ♠K, then ♠9, won by the ♠J,
South following with ♠3 - ♠6 - ♠8. How do you manage trumps?

(1) With no quick entry to dummy to utilise the diamond winners, you need to play trumps for just one loser. Given the overcall, North is more likely to hold the ♡A, but in that case you are doomed. If you lead ♡J from dummy, low from South, you play low and North wins with the ace, North can continue spades and enable South to over-ruff dummy on the fourth spade. To succeed, you have to find South with ♡A doubleton or either defender holding ♡Q singleton. Either way it is best to lead a low heart to your king at trick 2.

(2) The normal 2-1 trump split will see you home in this excellent slam. Most of the time it will be good enough to cash the top trumps but it costs next to nothing to cross to the ace of hearts and lead the jack of spades. You may be able to coax South to cover with the queen if South happens to have ♠Q-10-8. If South does cover, you capture the queen, return to dummy in hearts and take the marked finesse against the ♠10. Of course, if South does not cover the jack, you intend to rise with the ♠A and rely on the 2-1 break.

(3) The normal trump play is to cash the ♡A, ♡K but this could fail if South started with ♡Q-x-x and fewer than three diamonds. South could then ruff in when you start unblocking the diamonds and shift to spades. You might then lose three spades and the contract.

With six tricks in the minors, you need only four from the hearts. Best is to play a heart to the ace at trick 2, return to dummy with a club and lead the ♡J, playing low if South plays low. If this wins, you make at least one overtrick. If North began with ♡Q-x, the ♠K is safe from attack and you can use the fourth diamond for a spade pitch.

(4) How convenient! Why has North so kindly given you an entry to dummy? Although it is normal to finesse in clubs, be wary if North is a strong player. The likely motive for putting you into dummy is that North has the ♣K singleton. Beware of Greek gifts from good defenders. Trust players to base their actions on self-interest.

Chapter 4

OUT OF HARM'S WAY

So far the example hands have illustrated how trumps can be used to generate extra tricks for declarer. Of course, the defenders can also use their trumps to threaten declarer with extra losers. You must be alert to the dangers and ready to thwart their threats. If the task looks simple, always ask yourself what could go wrong.

♠ K Q J 7 4 3	N	♠ 10 9 8
♡ K 7	W E	♡ A 5 4 3 2
◇ K 8	S	◇ Q 6
♣ K 6 3		♣ A 4 2

Contract : 4♠.   Lead: ♡Q.

You have ten tricks with five spades, two hearts, one diamond and two clubs. You win with the king of hearts and lead a low spade. North wins with the ace and continues with the jack of hearts.

Is there any risk? What if hearts are 5-1? If the ace of hearts is ruffed, you have telescoped ten tricks into nine. Play low from dummy on the second heart and low again if a third heart is played, ruffing in hand. After drawing trumps, discard a club loser on the ♡A.

♠ A Q J 6	N	♠ K 10 7 4
♡ K 6 5 3	W E	♡ A J 4 2
◇ A 8	S	◇ 7 6
♣ K 6 3		♣ A 8 4

Contract : 4♡.   Lead: ♠9.

The danger is a spade ruff. You fail only if you lose two trump tricks. Cash the ♡A and ♡K and avoid the trump finesse. Even if North has ♡Q-10-x-x, you have just one trump loser by leading up to the ♡J.

Can you deal with the threatened ruff on this layout:

♠ A Q J 7 3
♡ A 6 2
◇ K 7 4
♣ A J

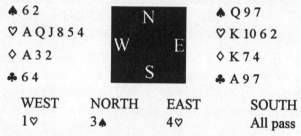

♠ K 10 6 4
♡ 7 4
◇ 9 8 6 5 3 2
♣ 6

Contract : 4♠. Lead: ◇ J.

South takes the ◇ A and returns the ◇ Q. How do you play?

You might fail if you instinctively cover the ◇ Q with the ◇ K and North ruffs. A heart switch will give the defence four tricks.

To guarantee ten tricks, all you need do is let the ◇ Q win. If the diamonds are 2-2 and South switches to hearts, you have escaped a diamond ruff. If South continues with the ◇ 10 and your ◇ K is ruffed, you have three established diamond winners in dummy.

♠ 6 2
♡ A Q J 8 5 4
◇ A 3 2
♣ 6 4

♠ Q 9 7
♡ K 10 6 2
◇ K 7 4
♣ A 9 7

WEST	NORTH	EAST	SOUTH
1♡	3♠	4♡	All pass

North leads the ace of spades and South plays the ♠5. Your move?

You need the ♠Q as a winner for a discard but unless you create some doubt, the ♠K will be cashed and the ♠Q ruffed at trick 3.

If you follow with the ♠2 at trick 1, North can tell that South's ♠5 is a singleton. However, if you play the ♠6, North cannot be sure who started with the singleton. Perhaps South's ♠5 is from ♠5-2. North might be afraid to play the ♠K, have it ruffed and set up the ♠Q as a winner. If North shifts to another suit, you can draw trumps and later lead up to your ♠Q.

Another unpleasant development is a threatened trump promotion.

♠ A Q 6 4 3   ♠ K 7 5 2
♡ Q J   ♡ 10 4 2
◊ A Q 10 7   ◊ K J 4
♣ 9 5   ♣ A 7 3

West is in 4♠. North starts with the ♡A, ♡K and a third heart. South ruffs dummy's ♡10 with the ten of spades. Your move?

Discard your inevitable club loser. That should be your last loser. If you over-ruff, you still have to lose a club later and a trump trick as well if North started with ♠J-9-8 or if South had ♠J-10-9-8.

♠ A 10 4 3   ♠ Q
♡ Q   ♡ J 9 6 5 4
◊ A K 10 9 6 5 ◊ J 8 7 4
♣ A 9   ♣ Q 4 2

Dealer South : Both vulnerable

WEST	NORTH	EAST	SOUTH
			1♡
Double	2♠	No	No
3◊	No	4◊	No
5◊	No	No	No

North, whose 2♠ jump shows a reasonable six-card suit and modest values, leads the ♡8. South wins with the king and shifts to the ◊2. You take the ◊A and North follows with the ◊3. What now?

The ♡8 lead marks South with A-K-10 in hearts. The ♣K is almost certainly there, too. Given North has six spades, you have a neat move. Draw the last trump, cash ♠A, ruff a spade, lead ♡J and when South covers with the king, discard a spade. South who started with ♠75 ♡A K 10 7 2 ◊Q 3 ♣K J 10 5 has to give dummy a trick in hearts or clubs, while you can ruff your last spade in dummy.

QUIZ 4

(1) *You*   *Dummy*

    ♠ K Q J 8   ♠ 10 9 6 4

    ♡ Q 8 2   ♡ A K 6

    ◇ A K  ◇ 8 5

    ♣ K 7 6 4   ♣ A 5 3 2

Contract : 4♠. Lead: ♣9. Plan the play.

(2) ♠ A Q 5   ♠ 9

    ♡ 6 4   ♡ 2

    ◇ A Q J  ◇ K 10 9 7 4 3

    ♣ K J 10 9 6   ♣ Q 8 7 5 2

Contract : 5♣ after North opened 1♠. *Lead:* ◇2. What is the danger? Can you circumvent it?

(3) ♠ A K Q   ♠ J 7 4 3

    ♡ K 10 3   ♡ J 7 4

    ◇ A  ◇ K 6

    ♣ A K 10 7 4 2   ♣ Q J 8 6

Contract : 6♣, after South opened 2♡, a weak two showing six hearts and 6-9 points. *Lead:* ♡2 to South's ace. Your move?

(4) ♠ Q 7   ♠ 6 4 2

    ♡ A Q J 7 4 3 2   ♡ K

    ◇ 8 4   ◇ A 9 6 3

    ♣ A K   ♣ 7 5 4 3 2

Contract : 4♡ after South opened 1♠. *Lead:* ♠9 to South's ♠K. South continues with the ♠A, followed by the ♠J.

(5)
♠ K Q J 7 3
♥ 9
♦ A J 10 6 3
♣ K 2

♠ 10 9 8 5
♥ A Q
♦ K Q 9 8 2
♣ 8 4

Dealer South : E-W vulnerable

WEST	NORTH	EAST	SOUTH
			1♡
1♠	4♡	4♠	5♡
5♠	No	No	Double
No	No	No	

Lead: ♣Q : four - three - king. How should you continue?

(6)
♠ - - -
♥ A J 10 9 8 4 2
♦ 8 5 2
♣ 10 9 5

♠ A J 10 9 3
♥ K Q
♦ A Q 3
♣ A 7 2

Contract : 6♡ after North opened 3♠. *Lead:* ♠K. Plan the play.

(7)
♠ K J 10
♥ K Q J 7 5 2
♦ 6
♣ 8 7 4

♠ 7 4 2
♥ 6 3
♦ A K 8 5 3 2
♣ J 10

Dealer South : Neither side vulnerable

WEST	NORTH	EAST	SOUTH
			1♣
1♡	1NT	2♦	2♠
3♡	No	No	No

Lead: ♣3. South takes the ♣Q, ♣K (North playing ♣9) and switches to the ace of spades followed by the ♠3. Your move?

[35]

(1) You have ten tricks, but beware. The threat of a club ruff is looming. When things are cosy, expect the worst and see what you can do about it. The fear here is that the ♣9 is a singleton. If you win the first club with dummy's ace and lead a spade, South might win and lead the queen of clubs. If your ♣K is ruffed, your ten winners have become nine.

As long as North ruffs a loser rather than a winner, you will be all right. The solution is easy enough. Win trick 1 in your own hand with the ♣K and start on trumps. If the lead was a singleton, the danger has evaporated.

(2) Clearly the ◇2 lead is a singleton. If South has the ♣A, you cannot escape the diamond ruff but North is more likely to have the ♣A for the opening bid. If you play a trump at trick 2, North can win and reach the South hand in hearts to receive the diamond ruff.

As North is a hot favourite to hold the king of spades on the bidding, you may be able to snip the defenders' communications by means of a 'scissors coup'. Take the ace of diamonds and continue with the ace of spades and the queen of spades. When North covers the queen, discard dummy's heart. If North does have the ♣A, there is no longer an entry to the South hand.

(3) You have little to lose by dropping the ♡K under the ace! If you do not, a heart ruff at trick 2 will certainly defeat you. If South is persuaded that your ♡K is singleton, he might switch for fear of setting up dummy's ♡J. If so, you will succeed comfortably.

(4) You can avoid the threatened trump promotion even if North began with four trumps and a doubleton spade. Discard your losing diamond on the third spade.

If South plays a fourth spade, ruff low in hand. If North over-ruffs, take this with dummy's ♡K, return to hand with a club and draw the rest of the trumps.

(5) Why did South fail to take the ♣A? Beware a defender who fails to take an ace at trick 1 in a trump contract. A ruff is imminent.

South's probable plan is to take the ♠A, play a club to North's jack and receive a diamond ruff. If South is competent, the diamond void is an odds-on favourite. In Chapter 8 you will see that East may have intended the double of 5♠ as a Lightner double, asking for an unusual lead in the hope that North could diagnose the diamond void.

Having spotted the problem, can you devise a solution? Your best move is a heart to the ace at trick 2 and continue with the ♡Q. If South covers with the ♡K as expected, discard your remaining club. This 'scissors coup' cuts out the entry to the North hand.

(6) There should be no problems as long as the ♠A is not ruffed at trick 1. While South is likely to have one spade, why take the risk? Play the ♠3 from dummy and ruff in hand. Draw trumps, cross to the ♣A and cash the ♠A, discarding a club. Continue with the ♠J and throw your remaining club. This loser-on-loser play gives North an unexpected trick with the ♠Q, but you have set up two spade winners in dummy and they will take care of your diamond losers.

(7) The bidding and play so far mark South with five clubs and four spades. North figures to have the ♡A and unless hearts are 3-2, you will have two heart losers to add to the three losers so far. You therefore need to assume that South is 4-2-2-5 with something like:

♠ A Q 5 3   ♡ 10 8   ◊ 7 4   ♣ A K Q 6 5

It is tempting to rise with the ♠K, ruff a club, cash the ◊A, ◊K to discard your spade loser and lead a trump but that will not work. North takes the ace of hearts and continues with a third diamond. South's ruff promotes a second trump winner for North. Therefore you cannot use dummy's second diamond winner. Your best chance is to finesse the jack of spades, ruff a club and lead a trump.

The defence might have defeated you a number of ways but you had no control in proceedings till trick 4. At that stage, you must play for a distribution that gives you a chance for success.

Chapter 5

IT'S UNDER CONTROL

You choose a trump suit to give you control of the play. Ideally you have significantly more trumps than they do, enabling you to draw their trumps while retaining some of your own. You may then be able to ruff their winners but they are unable to respond in kind.

Chapter 2 described how ruffing in the hand with fewer trumps often generates extra tricks while ruffing in the hand with more trumps usually gains little and may threaten your control of the play. You have seen some exceptions. Here is another kind:

♠ A K 10 9 8		♠ Q J 7
♡ K 9 4	N	♡ A 6 2
◇ 7	W E	◇ A 4 3 2
♣ A K 4 3	S	♣ Q J 10

Contract : 7♠. Lead: ◇K.

Twelve tricks are obvious but where is the thirteenth? A possible plan is to draw just two rounds of trumps. If they turn out to be 3-2, leave the last trump at large and cash four rounds of clubs, discarding a heart from dummy. You can then ruff the third heart in dummy. You need the hand with the last trump to hold at least four clubs, which is none too likely. Even if that works, you may find an early round of hearts is ruffed.

There is a better plan, known as 'dummy reversal' which requires no more than trumps breaking 3-2. The idea is to ruff three diamonds in your hand, thus making dummy the hand with more trumps with which you can draw the enemy trumps. Win the lead, ruff a diamond and draw two rounds of trumps with the ♠A and a trump to dummy's queen. If trumps are 3-2, ruff another diamond, re-enter dummy with a club and ruff the last diamond. A heart to the ace allows you to draw the last trump and claim thirteen tricks.

♠ A 8 6 5 4   ♠ 10 7 2
♡ 8   ♡ A 5 4 3
◇ Q 10 8 3   ◇ A K J 6
♣ A 5 2   ♣ 8 3

Contract : 4♠. Lead: ♠K.

On any other lead, your plan would be to ruff a club in dummy. The trump lead spells the end of this plan as it is all too likely that the moment you concede a club, an opponent will remove all of dummy's trumps, saddling you with four black losers.

A change of plans is necessary and the best bet is a dummy reversal. Duck the spade lead and win the likely trump continuation. Leave the last trump out and start ruffing dummy's hearts. A heart to the ace, heart ruff, diamond to the ace, heart ruff, diamond to the king and ruff dummy's last heart. Then cash your remaining diamond winners and the ace of clubs. If an opponent ruffs at any time, dummy's trump becomes a winner and if not, you have scored ten tricks.

You must learn to recognise when your trump control is threatened and try to find appropriate counter-measures. There is always some risk when you are playing in a 7-card fit, as one opponent figures to have four trumps. Six missing cards divide 4-2 much more often than 3-3.

♠ A Q J 10 8   ♠ K 9
♡ J   ♡ 7 4 3
◇ A 5 2   ◇ 7 6 4 3
♣ K Q J 10   ♣ A 9 6 3

Contract : 4♠. Lead: ♡A, followed by ♡K.

It would be careless to ruff at trick 2. Most of the time trumps will be 3-3 or 4-2 and your error will not cost, but if they are 5-1 (a one-in-seven chance) you will be in trouble. Correct is to discard the inevitable losers in diamonds on the third and fourth heart. A fourth heart can be ruffed in dummy, thus preserving your own 5-card holding.

Even when you have eight trumps, a 4-1 break can be a headache. Since the 4-1 break occurs about one time in four, you need to be conscious of the possibility and the risks presented by a 4-1 break.

♠ A K Q 7 3		♠ 10 9 2
♡ A 7 4 2		♡ 6 3
◊ K 8		◊ A Q J 10 9
♣ J 10		♣ 7 5 3

West plays 4♠ and North starts with the king and queen of clubs, followed by a club to South's ace. Your move?

You have eleven tricks if spades are 3-2 but suppose you ruff and cash your top spades, finding an opponent with J-x-x-x. If you play a fourth round of spades, the defender who wins may cash clubs. If you stop after three top trumps and start on diamonds, the defender with the last trump may ruff in by the fourth round, saddling you with one or more heart losers as there is no way back to dummy.

Count your tricks. As one ruff, three top spades, one heart and five diamonds total ten tricks, you can afford a trump loser. After ruffing the ♣Q, lead a low trump to dummy's ♠10. If this loses and clubs are continued, ruff in dummy, draw trumps and enjoy the diamonds.

♠ A 7 4 3 2		♠ K 6
♡ K 8 4		♡ A Q 5 2
◊ 6		◊ 8 5 3 2
♣ A K Q 2		♣ J 7 3

Against 4♠, North starts with ◊A and ◊K. How do you proceed?

You have to ruff the second diamond, otherwise you will have lost two tricks and the normal 4-2 trump break will saddle you with two more losers, and they will carry on with diamonds anyway. You should cash your two top spades but then abandon trumps and play your winners in the other suits. They can make their two trump tricks whenever they wish.

If you do try a third round of trumps, your partner may produce his version of the gripes of wrath if they play a fourth round of trumps, removing all of yours, and continue with their diamonds.

♠ A J 10 9 8   ♠ K Q 7
♡ A K Q J 10   ♡ 7
◇ - - -   ◇ 9 8 4 3
♣ A K Q   ♣ J 10 9 8 7

North leads a diamond against 7♠ but your pleasure at reaching this excellent contract is rudely interrupted when a spade to the king sees South discard a diamond. Can you survive this setback?

You plan to run hearts, for if North ruffs, you can over-ruff, draw trumps and your hand is high. What if North declines to ruff and discards clubs? North may then ruff when you play a club later. As you can discard only four clubs from dummy, cash one club before starting hearts. Now if North ruffs a heart, you are home and if not, you discard all of dummy's clubs and cross-ruff the rest of the tricks.

♠ A 9 8 2   ♠ 4
♡ K 8 5   ♡ A Q J 6
◇ A Q J 10 8   ◇ 7 5
♣ 2   ♣ A 8 7 6 5 4

Against 5◇, North leads the ♠K. You might succeed via ♠A, spade ruff, heart to king, spade ruff but that could lead to losing control of trumps later. It might work to win ♠A, cross to a heart and take the diamond finesse but if North ducks with ◇K-x-x or longer, you are in trouble. To prevent the defenders taking the ◇K and cashing spades, your best move, hard to see, is to duck the ♠K, retaining the ♠A for control. Ruff a spade continuation and start drawing trumps.

If North shifts to a trump at trick 2, win cheaply, ruff a spade, come to hand via the ♡K and continue with trumps. If North plays a heart at trick 2, win ♡K, ruff a spade and start on diamonds.

QUIZ 5

(1) *You*   *Dummy*

    ♠ A Q J 10   ♠ K 9 2

    ♡ 6 2   ♡ 7 5 4 3

    ◊ K 2   ◊ A 6 3

    ♣ A K Q J 10   ♣ 9 4 3

Contract : 4♠. Lead: ♡A, followed by the ♡K and a third heart to South's jack. Plan the play.

(2) ♠ K J 9 4   ♠ Q 10 8 5

    ♡ A K 7 4   ♡ 6 5 3 2

    ◊ K Q 10 4   ◊ A J 7 5

    ♣ A   ♣ 10

Contract : 4♡. Lead: ♣K. Will you finish with egg on your face?

(3) ♠ A 4   ♠ K 7 3 2

    ♡ A Q J 10 9   ♡ 8 7

    ◊ 8 6   ◊ 10 9 7

    ♣ A K Q J   ♣ 6 5 3 2

Contract : 4♡. Lead: ◊K followed by the ◊Q and the ◊J. How do you maximise your chances? Can you cope with a 4-2 trump break?

(4) ♠ Q J 10 9 6 4   ♠ 8 7

    ♡ A K   ♡ 8 5 3 2

    ◊ A K Q J   ◊ 8 6 3

    ♣ 4   ♣ K 10 6 3

Contract : 4♠. Lead: ♣Q. Can you foresee any problems? Will you be troubled by a 4-1 break in trumps?

(5)

♠ A 5 4 3 2		♠ K Q J
♡ 8 4		♡ A K 6 2
◊ - - -		◊ Q 7 4 3 2
♣ K Q J 10 9 8		♣ A

Contract : 6♠. Lead: ◊ J. Will you survive the 4-1 spade break?

(6)

♠ A K Q 10 9		♠ 8 3
♡ 6		♡ 7 5
◊ 9 6 2		◊ A K Q J 7 3
♣ A 7 5 2		♣ 10 4 3

Contract : 4♠. Lead: ♡A, followed by ♡K. Plan the play.

(7)

♠ 8 3		♠ J 6 2
♡ Q J 10 9 5		♡ K 6 4
◊ A J 5 4		◊ K Q 10
♣ A K		♣ 9 7 5 4

Dealer West : Neither side vulnerable

WEST	NORTH	EAST	SOUTH
1♡	No	1NT	No
2◊	No	3♡	No
4♡	No	No	No

Lead: ♠A, then ♠K and ♠Q. Can you cope if South has ♡A-x-x-x?

(8)

♠ - - -		♠ 9 7 5 4
♡ A K J 10 9		♡ Q 8 7 6
◊ A K Q J 10		◊ 9 8 7
♣ A K 6		♣ 9 4

Contract : 7♡. South opened 1♣ and bid 4♠ on the next round.
Lead: ♡2, on which South discards a club. Plan the play.

(1) A 4-3 trump fit is more likely to present 'control' problems than a 5-2 fit. If you reduce to three trumps in each hand, an opponent with four trumps may beat you. There is no value in refusing to ruff the third heart. A fourth heart leaves you with the same problem.

After ruffing, do not play three rounds of trumps. You will fail if either defender has four spades and four hearts. There is an easy solution. Cross to the ace of diamonds and ruff the fourth heart. Continue with ♠A and overtake the ♠Q with dummy's ♠K. Draw a third round of trumps with the ♠9 and then start clubs. If a defender who started with four spades ruffs in, the only possible return is a diamond, which is your entry to the rest of the clubs.

(2) You will survive cashing ace-king if trumps are 3-2 but if they are 4-1, you may find that the player with the ♠A cashes two more trumps, drawing yours, followed by clubs. Allowing an opponent to draw your trumps is a sure way to end with egg on your face.

The safe route is to cash just the ♡A and then force out the ♠A. The ♡K retains control of the trump suit. On regaining the lead, you draw a second round of trumps before playing off your side suit winners. Even a 4-1 trump break cannot hurt you now.

(3) Ruff the third diamond and lead the ♡Q. If this is taken by the king, you can ruff a diamond continuation in dummy.

If the ♡Q is allowed to win, cross to dummy with a spade and finesse the ♡J. If that wins, cash ♡A and abandon trumps. This caters for South holding four trumps. If the ♡J loses to the ♡K, you must hope that hearts are 3-3 or that North is out of diamonds.

(4) If you cover the ♣Q with the king, South may win and return a club. You must ruff and could now lose control if trumps are 4-1.

With North having the ♣J and South the ace, it is best to duck at trick 1. North cannot continue clubs without giving you a winner and, more importantly, a club guard to prevent your being forced to ruff.

(5) Ruff the diamond lead and cash the ♠K and ♠Q. If trumps break 3-2, no problems. If you find they are 4-1, unblock dummy's ♣A, then overtake the ♠K with your ♠A and continue clubs, then hearts. You lose one trump trick but retain control of the hand.

(6) You cannot afford to duck the second heart because a club switch could be fatal if an opponent has J-x-x-x in trumps. After ruffing, you should continue with the ♠10 to cater for a 4-2 trump break. A heart continuation can be ruffed in dummy, followed by a club to the ace. Then trumps are drawn, followed by the diamonds. You might even find North, with ♠J-x-x-x, ducking your ♠10.

(7) After ruffing the ♠Q, start with ♡Q and ♡J. If trumps are 3-2, your problems are over. Likewise if the ♡A has appeared. You can ruff a spade continuation with the ♡K, return to hand and draw the missing trump(s).

What if North shows out on the second heart and South ducks, remaining with ♡A-8? Should you continue hearts and hope South has no spades left? Hardly. As North would surely have overcalled 1♠ with ♠A-K-Q-x-x, South still has one or two spades. A better prayer is that South started with a 4-4-3-2 pattern. Try ♣A, ♣K, and ◇A, ◇K, ◇Q. If you have survived so far, cross-ruff the last tricks and lose one more only to the ♡A.

(8) It might work to play ♣A, ♣K and ruff your ♣6, but there is a danger. South's opening 1♣ and bidding 4♠ next with so little in high cards is surely at least a 6-5 pattern and quite possibly a 7-5. It should not be a huge shock if North ruffs a top club.

As North must have at least three diamonds, start with two rounds of diamonds. If South follows, South will be 5-0-2-6 and you can play to ruff a club. If South discards on the second diamond, cash two more diamonds discarding a club and play your last diamond. If North ruffs, over-ruff, cash the ♣A and cross-ruff the rest. If North does not ruff your last diamond, discard dummy's last club and again cross-ruff the rest.

Chapter 6

THE CARE AND HANDLING OF LOSERS

It's easy enough to deal with winners. Losers can also have an important role to play. How would you manage 4♡ on the ◊K lead?

♠ Q J 10 9 8		♠ 6 2
♡ A K J 8 4	N	♡ Q 10 7 6
◊ 8 6 4	W E	◊ A 7 3 2
♣ - - -	S	♣ K Q J

Shame about the diamond lead. On a trump lead you could have won in dummy and led the king of clubs. If South played low, you would have discarded a diamond, not caring whether you lost the trick or not, since you can afford to lose two spades and a club.

Now you must assume South has the ♣A. Win the lead and continue with the ♣K for a *ruffing finesse*. If South covers, you ruff, return to dummy with a trump and dump your losing diamonds on dummy's club winners. If South plays low on the ♣K, discard a diamond and pray that the ♣K wins.

♠ A 6		♠ 8 5 2
♡ 7 4 2	N	♡ 10 6 3
◊ A J 9 8 7 6 5 2	W E	◊ K Q 10
♣ - - -	S	♣ Q J 10 9

Against your awful 5◊, North leads the ♣4, South plays the ♣A and you ruff. Both follow when you lead a diamond to the king. What now?

A ruffing finesse in clubs is available if South has the ♣K but this is unlikely. With both ♣A and ♣K, it is normal to play the king at trick 1 in third seat. Still, leading the ♣Q and discarding a heart (a loser-on-loser play) will leave you one down at worst as you will not lose any spade tricks. Is that the best you can do?

You can display more imagination. If you discard a heart on the ♣Q, North will almost certainly be in a hurry to cash heart tricks before any more escape. Why not try a deceptive spade discard on the ♣Q?

Of course, you are risking an extra undertrick with this ruse, but experience with these situations indicates that defenders almost always try to cash tricks in the suit you are in a hurry to discard. If North does have the ♣K and shifts to a spade, two losing hearts go on the clubs. Your contract succeeds and the *post mortem* will be lively.

Loser-on-loser play can be helpful for a wide variety of reasons..

	♠ A K Q 2		♠ 7 4 3
♡ A K 5 4 3		♡ 9 8 7 6 2
♢ A 7		♢ J 9
♣ 6 5		♣ K 4 3

Dealer West : East-West vulnerable

WEST	NORTH	EAST	SOUTH
1♡	3♢ (1)	3♡	No
4♡	No	No	No

(1) Weak jump-overcall

North leads the king of diamonds which you capture. When you cash a top heart, North discards a diamond. You are in danger of losing one trump, one diamond and two clubs. All will be well if spades are 3-3 or the ♣A is onside but neither of these is likely in view of the bidding. Can you survive if neither black suit behaves?

Do not cash a second top trump. Play off the top spades. As North is unlikely to bid 3♢ with four spades, South will not ruff. If spades are 3-3, cash a top trump and discard a diamond on the last spade.

If South has four or more spades, you are all right, too. Play your last spade and discard dummy's diamond (loser-on-loser). If South exits with a trump, you win, ruff the diamond loser in dummy and exit with a trump. South wins but, with only clubs left, must give dummy a club trick. *Card Play Made Easy 1* has more endplay examples.

```
    ♠ A K Q J 2                    ♠ 6 5 4 3
    ♡ 7 3            N             ♡ 4
    ◇ K 4 3 2      W   E           ◇ 7 6 5
    ♣ A K            S             ♣ Q J 10 9 8
```

West plays 4♠ and North starts with the ace and king of hearts. If you ruff this in dummy and trumps are 3-1, you will be cut off from dummy's clubs. You will need the ace of diamonds onside as well as diamonds 3-3. That is asking for a lot.

You do not mind losing an extra heart trick to North as your ◇K is not threatened with North on lead. Discard the ◇5 on the second heart. If North plays a third heart, discard another diamond from dummy and ruff high in your own hand. Draw trumps, unblock the clubs and reach dummy's club winners with the ♠2 to dummy's ♠6.

Another problem you may encounter is to safeguard your ruff in dummy without running into an over-ruff.

```
    ♠ A Q J 10 9                   ♠ K 5 3
    ♡ A              N             ♡ 8 7 5 4 3 2
    ◇ A K 6 4 3    W   E           ◇ 7 5
    ♣ A 3            S             ♣ 7 5
```

Against 6♠, North leads the ♣K. You win, cash ◇A, ◇K and ruff the ◇3 with the ♠K. If North began with four diamonds, return to hand with a heart and discard dummy's ♣7 on your fourth diamond. Your last diamond is high and you ruff your club loser in dummy.

```
    ♠ A K Q J 10 9                 ♠ 4 3 2
    ♡ A 6            N             ♡ J 2
    ◇ 7 4 3 2      W   E           ◇ 9 6 5
    ♣ A             S             ♣ 6 5 4 3 2
```

Against 3♠, North starts with four top diamonds. Your move?

If you ruff, South will over-ruff and you will lose a heart later for one down. All you need do is throw dummy's ♡2 on the fourth diamond. You can ruff a heart in dummy with virtually no risk. North might have done better by shifting to hearts earlier.

♠ A 9 6 3 2
♡ K 5
◊ Q J 8 7 4 3
♣ - - -

♠ 7 5 4
♡ - - -
◊ A K 6 5 2
♣ A Q 6 5 2

Against 6◊, North leads the queen of hearts. Your plan?

Before making any move, you should pause for thought. If instead of the automatic ruff, you discard a spade from dummy (loser-on-loser), South will win but your ♡K is now high for another spade discard. Exchanging a heart loser for two spade losers cannot be bad business.

Can you spot the problem on this layout? You are in 6♡ and receive a diamond lead.

♠ A 5 3
♡ A Q J 10 9
◊ A
♣ A K 10 8

♠ 6 4 2
♡ K 7 3
◊ J 6
♣ Q 6 4 3 2

The problem which will concern you later is why you are not in 7♣. The problem here and now is the potential blockage in clubs. There seem to be twelve tricks via five hearts, five clubs and two aces but if either opponent has ♣J-x-x, after you cash your three top clubs, the remaining club in your hand will block the suit.

The solution is pretty, an elegant 'winner-on-loser' play. Take the ◊A, draw three rounds of trumps ending in dummy and play the ◊J. On this you discard the ♣8, eliminating the blockage and ensuring your slam unless the clubs are 4-0.

QUIZ 6

(1) *You*   *Dummy*

   ♠ 9   ♠ A 8 7 5

   ♡ A J 5   ♡ 6 4 2

   ◊ Q J 2   ◊ - - -

   ♣ A Q 7 6 5 3   ♣ K J 10 9 4 2

Contract : 6♣. Lead: ◊ 3. Plan the play.

(2) ♠ A Q 10 7 5 4 2   ♠ K J 8 3

   ♡ Q J 10   ♡ A 9 5

   ◊ K 7   ◊ 8 4 3

   ♣ 4   ♣ K Q 2

Dealer North : Neither side vulnerable

WEST	NORTH	EAST	SOUTH
	No	1NT	No
4♠	No	No	No

North leads the jack of clubs. What is your best line?

(3) ♠ A 9 5 3   ♠ K 6 2

   ♡ A K Q J 10 9   ♡ 6 5 4

   ◊ A 2   ◊ 8 3

   ♣ 2   ♣ J 10 6 4 3

Contract : 4♡. Lead: ♠Q. Nine tricks are there. Where is the tenth?

(4) ♠ K J 10 4 3 2   ♠ 7 5

   ♡ 10 6   ♡ A K 4 2

   ◊ 8 7 6   ◊ A 5 3

   ♣ 4 2   ♣ A K Q 7

Contract : 4♠. Lead: ◊Q. Can you make this if North has ♠A-Q?

(5)

♠ A K Q 9 7 5 3		♠ J 10
♡ 9 4 2		♡ A Q 10 7
◇ 8		◇ K Q 10 9
♣ 6 3		♣ 7 5 4

Dealer North : Neither side vulnerable

WEST	NORTH	EAST	SOUTH
	No	1NT	No
4♠	No	No	No

North starts with the ♣A, ♣K and ♣Q. Plan your play.

(6)

♠ 7		♠ J 6
♡ A K J 7 5		♡ Q 10 9
◇ K 8 6		◇ Q J 10 9
♣ 8 6 4 3		♣ A K 5 2

Contract : 4♡. *Lead:* ♠A, followed by ♠K. Plan the play.

(7)

♠ A J 2		♠ K 6 3
♡ A Q 10 3 2		♡ K 6 5 4
◇ 7 5 3		◇ 10 4
♣ K 3		♣ A 7 5 4

Contract : 4♡. *Lead:* ◇K, taken by South with the ace. South returns the ◇J to North's queen. Next comes the ◇9. Well?

(8)

♠ K J 9 8 6 4 3		♠ A Q 10
♡ J		♡ A 10 9 8
◇ 8 3		◇ A Q 5
♣ A K 7		♣ 8 6 5

Contract : 6♠. *Lead:* ◇7. Plan the play.

(1) Your best chance is that North has led away from the ◊K. Discard the ♡2 from dummy and if South wins with the ◊A, you have some cause for optimism. Take the heart return with the ace, draw the missing trump and take a ruffing finesse in diamonds. If North does have the ◊K, you will be able to discard dummy's other heart loser.

(2) If you make the reasonable assumption that South has the ace of clubs, you can virtually guarantee the contract provided that you play low from dummy at trick 1. If South overtakes with the ace and shifts to diamonds, you may lose a club and two diamonds, but you will be spared the heart finesse. You can discard two hearts on dummy's ♣K-Q.

It is more likely that South will let the ♣J win. If North then switches to a heart, rise with the ace, draw trumps ending in dummy and take a ruffing finesse in clubs. You later discard a diamond on dummy's club winner and lose one heart, one diamond and one club.

If you cover the ♣J at trick 1, South can take the ♣A and switch to diamonds. If you lose two diamonds and the heart finesse is off, you have just failed in a laydown game.

(3) Take the ♠K and ♠A and concede a spade. If the spades are not 3-3, you plan to discard a diamond on the fourth spade and ruff a diamond in dummy. Note that drawing even one round of trumps first could be fatal, as the above play might allow the defenders the opportunity to play two more rounds of trumps.

(4) You start by winning the ◊A and playing the top clubs to discard one diamond. If you now take a trump finesse, there are a number of ways you might be defeated. Suppose North started with:

♠ A Q 9   ♡ 8 5 3   ◊ Q J 10   ♣ 10 8 6 5

North can win the first spade, cash one diamond and then play the fourth club. If South ruffs with the ♠8, North scores three trump tricks to put you one down. Similarly, if North originally had:

♠ A Q 9   ♡ 8 5 3   ◊ Q J 10 4   ♣ 8 6 5

North could win the first spade, play a diamond to South and the fourth club from South promotes an extra trump winner for North. To minimise the risk of succumbing to a trump promotion, it is best to play dummy's fourth club and discard your last diamond.

(5) Had North switched to a heart earlier, you were a goner but now you are safe. Ruff the club and lead a diamond to dummy's 9. As North passed as dealer and has shown up with 9 HCP in clubs, the ◊A must be with South. Even if South wins with the ◊J, all is well. If South exits with a trump, win with the ♠10 in dummy, draw a second round with the ♠J and take a ruffing finesse in diamonds.

(6) If you ruff the ♠K and play two rounds of trumps, you could be in trouble if hearts are 4-1. If you switch to diamonds and they are 4-2, the defender with ◊A-x-x-x might duck the first diamond, win the second and play a third for partner to ruff. With a club still to be lost, you are one down. To avoid such possible unpleasantness, pitch a club on the ♠K (and another one later on the fourth diamond).

(7) South's play smacks of ◊A-J doubleton. If you ruff low, South might over-ruff. If you ruff high, you might find North now has a trump trick with ♡J-x-x (and South did not start with a doubleton diamond after all!). In either case, you figure to fail if the spade finesse loses. The safest move is to discard a spade from dummy on the third diamond and later ruff a spade in dummy.

(8) Taking the diamond finesse is at best a 50% chance. There is a far better play, especially as North would probably have led the ♡K from a holding headed by ♡K-Q. Rise with the ◊A, cash the ♡A and lead the ♡10. If South plays low, discard the diamond loser and later take a ruffing finesse in hearts to dispose of your club loser.

If South covers the ♡10, you ruff, play two rounds of trumps ending in dummy and continue with the ♡9, throwing the diamond loser unless South produces the missing heart honour. If North wins, you have set up a heart winner in dummy for your club loser.

Chapter 7

EXTENSIONS AND REDUCTIONS

One of the most profitable uses for trumps is to create extra winners from a modest but extended suit in dummy. You need enough entries in dummy not only to set up the winners but also to return to dummy to cash them. This is typical:

♠ J		♠ A 8 7 5 4 3
♡ A Q J 9 5 3 2	N	♡ K 10
◇ 10 4 2	W E	◇ A 8 6
♣ Q 6	S	♣ J 5

Against your ambitious 4♡, the defence takes two clubs and shifts to a diamond. How do you propose to justify your bidding?

Nine winners are obvious. The tenth must come from spades. You will need not only luck but the skill to benefit from your luck. Take the ◇A, continue with ♠A and a spade ruff. After a low heart to the ten, ruff another spade. If spades are 3-3, half your worries are over as the spades in dummy are winners. Lead a heart to the king and if trumps are 2-2, you are home. Cash your spades, discarding your losers, and commiserate with the opponents about their rotten luck. Note that even one round of trumps before starting on the spades would have been fatal. Dummy would then be one entry short.

♠ J		♠ A 8 7 5 4 3
♡ A Q J 9 5 3 2	N	♡ K 8
◇ 10 4 2	W E	◇ A 8 6
♣ Q 6	S	♣ J 5

After the same start by the defence, this 4♡ needs even more luck. After ♠A and a spade ruff, you need to finesse the ♡8 in order to create the extra entry needed for success.

When setting up a long suit, certain precautions are essential:

♠ 7 6
♥ 8 3
◊ A K 2
♣ A Q J 7 6 5

♠ A K 5 3 2
♥ 9 7
◊ 8 6 4
♣ K 10 3

Against 5♣, the defenders cash two hearts and switch to a trump. How do you manage this?

You have ten tricks on top and need to set up one extra spade trick. If spades break 4-2, the most common split, the plan is ♠A, ♠K, ruff a spade, cross to the ♣10, ruff another spade, cross to the ♣K and cash the fifth spade for a diamond discard. The first important point is to win the trump switch in your hand to preserve the ♣K and ♣10 as entries to dummy. For the same reason, you must not play another round of trumps yet. After ♠A, ♠K and a third spade, if South follows, make sure you ruff high. It is silly to be over-ruffed when you can afford a high ruff. Finally if spades happen to be 3-3, make sure all the trumps have been drawn before you try to cash a spade.

Sometimes you may have a choice of plays.

♠ J 3
♥ 8
◊ K J 2
♣ A Q 9 8 7 6 2

♠ A Q 4
♥ A 9 6 5 3
◊ Q 6
♣ K J 10

North leads the ♠5 against 6♣. Where is your twelfth trick?

One plan is to take the spade finesse. If it works, you are home. It is better to play to set up hearts. Win ♠A, cash ♥A, ruff a heart, cross to ♣10, ruff a heart, cross to ♣J, ruff a heart. If the hearts are 4-3, dummy's last heart is good. Cross to the ♣K and discard your spade loser on the fifth heart, then knock out the ◊A. The chance of a 4-3 break in hearts (62%) is better than the spade finesse (50%).

Skilful play can sometimes overcome a bad break in the trump suit but you need to know the technique involved.

♠ Q 10 8 7 4 3	N	♠ A K
♡ 9 7 3	W E	♡ 8 6 4 2
◊ K J 2	S	◊ A Q 6
♣ 7		♣ A K Q 3

West plays 4♠ and North starts with the ace, king and queen of hearts, all following, then switches to a diamond. Where do you win this? On the ♠A, both follow low but on the ♠K, North discards a diamond. Can you overcome this misfortune?

South began with ♠J-x-x-x and the only way to cope with such a situation is to reduce your trump length to the same as South's and ensure that the lead is not in your own hand at trick 12. Win the diamond shift in hand with ◊K, cash ♠A, ♠K, cash ♣A and ruff a club (first reduction), cross to ◊Q, ruff a club (second reduction). You are now down to ♠Q-10. Play a diamond to the ace and if South cannot ruff this you are all right. Whatever you lead from dummy, South has to play a trump from ♠J-x and you over-ruff.

Sometimes you need to take a precautionary move before you discover that a bad break exists.

♠ 7 4	N	♠ A K 3
♡ 5	W E	♡ A 6 4 3 2
◊ 8 2	S	◊ A K 7 5
♣ A K Q 9 8 7 5 3		♣ 10

You are in the excellent contract of 7♣ and North leads the king of hearts. How do you proceed?

There is good news and bad news. The good news is that you have avoided 7NT which would be doomed when the bad news turns up: South started with all four trumps. Can you cope with this?

If you took the ♡A and led the ♣10 to your ace, the good news has ended. South has ♣J-x-x left and you need to come down to the same trump length. To reduce by ruffing four times and then return to dummy requires five entries but you can reach dummy only four times. When you come down to ♣K-Q-9, you will be in your hand.

To succeed you need to have taken the far-sighted precaution of ruffing a heart at trick 2 *just in case South started with ♣J-x-x-x.* The play goes ♡A, heart ruff, ♣A, diamond to ace, heart ruff, diamond to king, heart ruff, spade to ace, heart ruff, spade to king. If South has not ruffed, you will bask in partner's adulation for days.

On this deal, an expert playing in 4♠ miraculously condensed four losers into three after West started with ace and king of clubs.

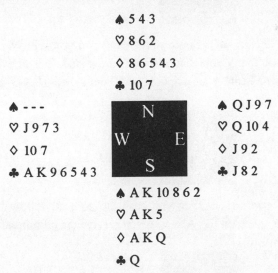

```
              ♠ 5 4 3
              ♡ 8 6 2
              ◇ 8 6 5 4 3
              ♣ 10 7
♠ - - -                        ♠ Q J 9 7
♡ J 9 7 3        N             ♡ Q 10 4
◇ 10 7       W       E         ◇ J 9 2
♣ A K 9 6 5 4 3     S          ♣ J 8 2
              ♠ A K 10 8 6 2
              ♡ A K 5
              ◇ A K Q
              ♣ Q
```

South ruffed the ♣K with the ♠6 (remarkable foresight) and the ♠A revealed the bad break. After three diamonds and three hearts, East was in with the ♡Q. He led the ♠Q, but South played ♠8, leaving East on lead. East switched to a club but South ruffed with the ♠2 and over-ruffed with dummy's ♠5. He now had the ♠K-10 poised over East's ♠J-9 with the lead in dummy.

QUIZ 7

(1) *You*   *Dummy*

      ♠ A   ♠ 7 5 4 3 2

      ♡ A Q   ♡ 6 4 2

      ◊ K 7 2   ◊ A Q J

      ♣ A Q J 9 6 5 3   ♣ K 10

Contract : 7♣. Lead: ◊ 5. Plan the play.

(2) ♠ A K Q 9 8 7 6 5   ♠ - - -

      ♡ A 2   ♡ K 4 3

      ◊ 5 2   ◊ A K 8 6

      ♣ A   ♣ 8 7 5 4 3 2

Contract : 6♠. Lead: ♣Q. South plays the 9 and you win. When you cash ♠A, you thank your lucky stars you avoided 7NT and 7♠ as North discards a heart. Can you deal with South's ♠J-10-4-3-2?

(3) ♠ A   ♠ 7 5 4

      ♡ A 8   ♡ K Q 9 4 3 2

      ◊ 5 4 2   ◊ A K J

      ♣ A K Q 10 9 8 7   ♣ 6

Contract : 7♣. Lead: ♠K. When you cash the ♣A, all follow but North discards a spade on the ♣K. Can you survive the club break?

(4) ♠ K Q 9 8 4 2   ♠ A J 10

      ♡ 10 5   ♡ 8 7 6 4 3

      ◊ A K 5   ◊ 8 6 3

      ♣ A 2   ♣ J 6

Contract : 4♠. Lead: ◊ Q. Reverse East's length in the minor suits and this would be a cinch. As it is, you are in danger of losing four tricks. What can you do to overcome this?

(5) ♠ K Q 3
  ♡ A K
  ◇ A 10 9 8 7 6
  ♣ 6 3

  ♠ A 9 4
  ♡ Q J 7 2
  ◇ K Q
  ♣ 7 5 4 2

Contract : 5◇ after South opened 1♣. *Lead:* ♣10, taken by South's jack. South cashes the ♣Q, North playing ♣8. South continues with the ♣A. What do you do? Decide before reading further.

If you have chosen to ruff low, you are still alive. When you cash ◇K, ◇Q, North discards a heart on the second round. How do you plan the play from this point?

(6) ♠ A K Q J 9 2
  ♡ A 5
  ◇ 5 4
  ♣ Q J 10

  ♠ 5 4
  ♡ Q 10 9
  ◇ A 8 6 3 2
  ♣ A K 5

Contract : 6♠. *Lead:* ♠6, South plays ♠10. Plan the play.

(7) ♠ K 2
  ♡ A J 10 5 3 2
  ◇ 7 6 4
  ♣ K 3

  ♠ A Q J 3
  ♡ K 4
  ◇ 9 8 2
  ♣ A Q J 10

Contract : 4♡. *Lead:* ◇A, ◇K, ◇Q, followed by a spade switch. All follow to the king of hearts but North discards a club when you lead a heart to the jack. How do you continue?

(8) ♠ 6 4
  ♡ A 9 7 5 3 2
  ◇ A Q 7 4
  ♣ A
  ♠ A K 5 3
  ♡ Q J
  ◇ K 10 2
  ♣ K 7 4 2

Contract : 6♡. *Lead:* ♠Q. Can you deal with South's ♡K-10-8-6?

(1) With twelve tricks on top, the thirteenth can come from the heart finesse or by setting up an extra trick in spades. In such cases, always try first the line that does not lose the lead. Win with the ◇K, cash ♠A, cross to ♣10 and ruff a spade high, cross to ♣K and ruff another spade high. With a choice of entries to dummy, use the entries in the trump suit first. Now draw any trumps still outstanding.

After two spade ruffs, you will know whether the spades were 4-3 originally. If so, cross to ◇Q, ruff a spade, cross to ◇A and cash the fifth spade to discard the ♡Q. If spades were 5-2, cross to dummy in diamonds and take the heart finesse. There is a squeeze option but this is no better than the heart finesse.

(2) After the bad break is revealed, you need to reduce your trumps to the same length as South's trumps. Cross to the ◇A, ruff a club, cash ♡A, ♡K and ruff a club, followed by a diamond to the king and ruff once more. You will be all right as long as South has not ruffed any of your winners as you are now down to ♠K-Q-9-8. Exit with the ♠8. South wins but has to lead a trump from the remaining ♠J-x-x, allowing you to finesse the ♠9.

(3) After ♠A, ♣A, ♣K, revealing the bad break, you need four entries to dummy: three to reduce your trumps to the same length as South and one to return to dummy at trick 12. That means you will have to risk the diamond finesse at some stage.

Cash ♡A, cross to ♡K and ruff a spade. Play a diamond to the ace and ruff another spade. Finesse the ◇J, ruff a heart and finally cross to the ◇K. If you have survived till now, you are left with ♣Q-10 and with the lead in dummy, the value of South's ♣J-5 is negated.

(4) The only hope for an extra trick is to set up at least one winner in hearts but you must start the hearts at once. Take the ace of diamonds and lead a heart. If the opponents switch to a trump, win and lead another heart. You now succeed only if the hearts are 3-3.

On the other hand, if the opponents take the heart and say, continue diamonds, you will succeed even if hearts are 4-2. Take the diamond and lead another heart. When you regain the lead, cross to dummy in spades and ruff a heart. If hearts are 3-3, dummy's hearts are high. If there is still one heart out, return to dummy in spades, ruff another heart, return to dummy in spades to cash the last heart.

Do not play one round of trumps. If you do and spades are 3-1, they can beat you even if hearts are 3-3. After the ace of diamonds, spade cashed, heart conceded, they can play a second trump, and another one on winning the second heart. Now there is no way back later to dummy even if the hearts come good.

(5) Ruff the third club low. If you ruff with the ◊A, you succeed only if the jack of diamonds falls singleton or doubleton. Even without any opposition bidding, the percentage play is to ruff low. As South opened the bidding, South is highly likely to have the ◊J.

When the ◊K, ◊Q reveals South started with ◊J-x-x-x, you need to bring your trumps down to South's trump length. As you have ruffed once, one more ruff will do it. Ruff a club and cash the ♡A, ♡K. Then cross to the spade ace and lead dummy's heart winners. If South ruffs, you can over-ruff. If South discards, you discard your spades and a spade from dummy at trick 12 finishes the coup.

You succeed as long as South began with a 2-2-4-5 or a 1-3-4-5 pattern. You cannot succeed if South has fewer than two hearts but it is important not to play two rounds of spades. That would be fatal if South started with a singleton spade.

(6) You have two choices: play for an extra trick in hearts (ace and another is as good as any other move in hearts) or play to set up an extra diamond trick. The heart play is a bit better than 50% since a singleton honour with either player or a doubleton jack or king with North eliminates any guess, but playing to set up a diamond trick has over 80% chance of success. Once you elect to go for diamonds, draw the remaining trumps and discard hearts from dummy.

The whole deal might be:

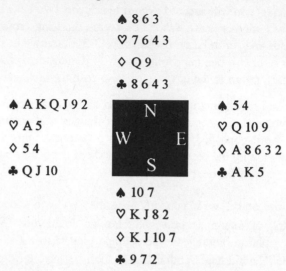

```
                 ♠ 8 6 3
                 ♡ 7 6 4 3
                 ◇ Q 9
                 ♣ 8 6 4 3
♠ A K Q J 9 2          N          ♠ 5 4
♡ A 5             W         E     ♡ Q 10 9
◇ 5 4                  S          ◇ A 8 6 3 2
♣ Q J 10                          ♣ A K 5
                 ♠ 10 7
                 ♡ K J 8 2
                 ◇ K J 10 7
                 ♣ 9 7 2
```

After three rounds of spades, discarding a heart from dummy, play a low diamond from both hands. With only two entries in dummy outside diamonds, starting the diamonds with ace and another can cost. You would survive with diamonds 3-3, but if they are 4-2, you cross to dummy with a club, ruff a diamond, club to dummy and ruff a diamond, setting up the fifth diamond. One tiny snag: you cannot return to dummy to reach the winner.

Ducking the first round of diamonds provides the extra, essential entry. If they win and switch to clubs, make sure you win this in your own hand. Then ace of diamonds, ruff a diamond, cross in clubs and ruff the fourth round of diamonds. You now return to dummy with a club to cash the diamond and discard the ♡5.

(7) You must reduce your trump length to the same as South. Play a spade to dummy, ruff a spade, club to dummy, ruff a spade, club to dummy and if South has not ruffed a winner, you are in dummy with ♡A-10 in hand ready to pick off South's ♡Q-x. The fact that you are ruffing winners is incidental to the main aim of trump reduction.

(8) You can hardly fail to make your slam if trumps break 3-2. Can you do anything to overcome a possible 4-1 split in hearts. The full deal looked like this:

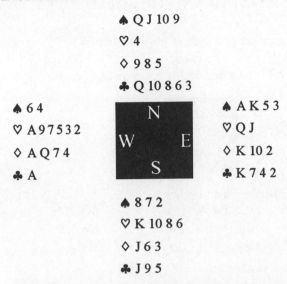

```
                    ♠ Q J 10 9
                    ♡ 4
                    ◊ 9 8 5
                    ♣ Q 10 8 6 3
    ♠ 6 4                           ♠ A K 5 3
    ♡ A 9 7 5 3 2       N           ♡ Q J
    ◊ A Q 7 4        W     E        ◊ K 10 2
    ♣ A                 S           ♣ K 7 4 2
                    ♠ 8 7 2
                    ♡ K 10 8 6
                    ◊ J 6 3
                    ♣ J 9 5
```

Declarer won the spade lead with dummy's ace and unblocked the ace of clubs. He then led a low heart to dummy's queen which held. It makes no difference if South wins the first heart.

Next came the ♣K, discarding a diamond, followed by a club ruff. A heart to the jack was won by South and the spade return went to dummy's king. After a spade ruff and three rounds of diamonds ending in dummy, declarer had ♡A-9 over South's ♡10-8.

Note that because the spade lead has taken an entry out of dummy, you cannot succeed if you win the ♠A and continue with the queen of hearts, ducked, and the jack of hearts, covered by the king. You now fail whether you capture South's king or not.

Suppose after ♠A, ♣A and a heart to the queen, South wins and returns a spade to the king. Cash ♣K, ruff a club, cross to ♡J, ruff a spade, and finish proceedings with three diamonds, ending in dummy.

Chapter 8

UNNATURAL AND DEVILISH ACTS

This final chapter takes a look at plays which do not fit naturally elsewhere. While some are exotic and can be admired for their elegance, the problem on this deal is common enough.

♠ A		♠ J 4
♡ A K 7 5 4 3	N	♡ Q J 10 6
◇ A J	W E	◇ K 4
♣ 6 5 3 2	S	♣ A Q J 8 4

Dealer East : Both vulnerable

WEST	NORTH	EAST	SOUTH
		1♣	No
2♡	No	3♡	No
3♠	No	4♣	No
4◇	No	4♡	No
6♡	No	No	Double
No	No	No	

North leads the 7 of clubs. How should you play?

In the same contract on the same lead but without the double, you should rise with the ♣A. If the lead is a singleton, it would be silly to finesse the queen, lose, and find that North ruffs the club return.

Does South's double change that? The slam is excellent and South can hardly be expecting to beat it with isolated kings and queens. No, South's double is conventional, the *Lightner double*, asking for an unusual lead. Normally, the Lightner double asks for the lead of dummy's first bid suit, often because the doubler is void in that suit.

If you deduce that South is void in clubs, you can see that it would be fatal to play the ♣A. Indeed, even the ♣Q or ♣J would spell defeat if South ruffs. You must find the unnatural play of the ♣8!

North made it tough for you by leading the 7 from ♣K-10-9-7. The lead of the 10 would have been less of a problem. If you play the queen or jack on the 7, South ruffs and you will still lose a club trick later. When you play the ♣8, South can ruff, but you win any return, draw the missing trumps and finesse twice in clubs to make your doubled slam.

Sometimes you may need to delve into an opponent's mind, especially if they seem to have made an obvious blunder.

♠ A K Q J 4		♠ 10 9 8 7 5
♡ 9 5 3	N	♡ A K
◊ 6 5 2	W E	◊ K J 10 9
♣ Q 9	S	♣ J 8

Against your 4♠, North starts with the ace and king of clubs. To your surprise, North plays the ♣10 at trick 3. Your plan?

By all means accept the ruff and discard, ruffing in dummy and discarding a losing diamond, but ask yourself why North has played the third club when a perfectly safe exit in hearts was available. You should always be wary of a defender who gives you a way of playing for your contract that was not available all along. Trust an opponent to be operating primarily out of self-interest.

North has in fact made a risky play. If you had held only two diamonds, North's play might have given you the contract. Why would North do that?

We believe that North has the queen of diamonds but not the ace and is trying to provide you with the losing option of playing a diamond to dummy's king. Do not be misled. Draw trumps and play a diamond to the jack as you would have done if North had exited with a heart at trick 3.

Perhaps you consider this reasoning as evidence of advanced paranoia in the authors, but it is worth remembering that just because you are paranoid does not mean they are not out to get you.

The trump suit itself is rarely the centrepiece of a squeeze but using the trump suit can increase your chances. If it appears that success depends essentially on a favourable break in a side suit, it can often pay you to play off all your trumps first. Not only may the defenders err in their discarding but a squeeze might develop. Even if you are not familiar with squeeze play, playing off all your trumps will not harm you if they are not needed for other purposes. Take a look at this problem:

♠ A K Q J 10 9	**N**	♠ 8 6
♡ A K Q 2	**W E**	♡ 7 6 4 3
◇ 5	**S**	◇ A 6 2
♣ K 6		♣ A 7 4 3

Dealer North : Both vulnerable

WEST	NORTH	EAST	SOUTH
	3◇	No	No
Double	No	4♡	No
4NT	No	5♡	No
7♠	No	No	No

North leads the king of diamonds. How would you tackle the play?

Since there will be no problem if hearts are 3-2, declarer should assume that the hearts break badly. Even if South has four or five hearts, you have a good chance and this becomes a certainty if, as expected, North started with at least seven diamonds.

At this point, South figures to have another diamond. To eliminate that, you win the ace of diamonds and ruff a diamond at trick 2. This should leave North as the only one guarding the diamonds. Dummy's last diamond is a 'threat' because North cannot afford to discard all his diamonds without giving you a diamond winner. Ruffing the diamond at trick 2 is called 'isolating the menace'.

You now draw trumps and cash the ♡A, ♡K, ♡Q. If the hearts do not break, continue by playing trumps. The full deal could be:

```
              ♠ 4 3
              ♡ 8
              ◇ K Q J 10 8 7 3
              ♣ Q J 8
♠ A K Q J 10 9              ♠ 8 6
♡ A K Q 2         N        ♡ 7 6 4 3
◇ 5            W     E      ◇ A 6 2
♣ K 6             S         ♣ A 7 4 3
              ♠ 7 5 2
              ♡ J 10 9 5
              ◇ 9 4
              ♣ 10 9 5 2
```

After ◇A, diamond ruff, ♠A, ♠K, ♠Q (discarding a heart), ♡A, ♡K, ♡Q, followed by the ♠J (discarding a club), the position is:

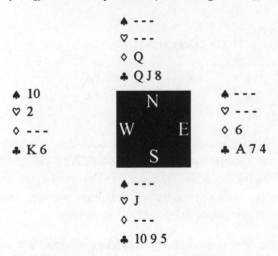

```
              ♠ - - -
              ♡ - - -
              ◇ Q
              ♣ Q J 8
♠ 10                       ♠ - - -
♡ 2            N           ♡ - - -
◇ - - -     W     E        ◇ 6
♣ K 6             S        ♣ A 7 4
              ♠ - - -
              ♡ J
              ◇ - - -
              ♣ 10 9 5
```

On the ♠10, North must keep a diamond and so throws the ♣8. You now discard dummy's ◇6 (it was vital not to throw it earlier) and South must let go a heart or a club. Either way you make the rest.

Squeezes can work just as well in no-trumps simply by running a long suit but the squeeze on the following deal cannot operate without a trump suit. Fittingly it is called a 'ruffing squeeze'.

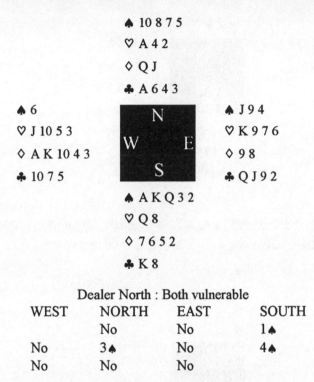

```
              ♠ 10 8 7 5
              ♡ A 4 2
              ◇ Q J
              ♣ A 6 4 3
♠ 6                              ♠ J 9 4
♡ J 10 5 3                       ♡ K 9 7 6
◇ A K 10 4 3                     ◇ 9 8
♣ 10 7 5                         ♣ Q J 9 2
              ♠ A K Q 3 2
              ♡ Q 8
              ◇ 7 6 5 2
              ♣ K 8
```

Dealer North : Both vulnerable

WEST	NORTH	EAST	SOUTH
	No	No	1♠
No	3♠	No	4♠
No	No	No	

West starts with the ace and king of diamonds, East signalling high-then-low to ask for diamonds to be continued. West obliges by playing the ◇3. You try the ♠10 in dummy, but East over-ruffs with the jack. When East exits with a trump, you draw the remaining trumps and ruff your remaining diamond loser in dummy.

In other circumstances, you might try to endplay an opponent into leading away from the king of hearts. As you have already lost three tricks, a throw-in play is not a good idea. Instead you return to hand with a club to the king. This leaves the following position:

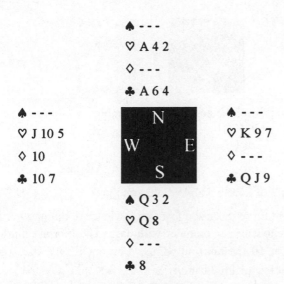

```
          ♠ - - -
          ♡ A 4 2
          ◊ - - -
          ♣ A 6 4

♠ - - -       N        ♠ - - -
♡ J 10 5             ♡ K 9 7
◊ 10     W       E   ◊ - - -
♣ 10 7       S        ♣ Q J 9

          ♠ Q 3 2
          ♡ Q 8
          ◊ - - -
          ♣ 8
```

Even at this stage it is not easy to see how South can avoid losing a heart trick but see what happens when South plays two more rounds of trumps, discarding two hearts from dummy. East can discard one heart but has no good move after that.

If East discards another heart to come down to ♡K singleton, you can play off dummy's ace of hearts, dropping the king, cash the ♣A, ruff a club to reach your hand and the winning queen of hearts.

If East discards a club in order to keep K-x in hearts, you can cash the ace of clubs and ruff a club. This removes the clubs held by the opponents and leaves dummy's last club as a winner. You return to dummy with a heart to enjoy the low club as your tenth trick. This ruffing aspect in clubs explains the 'ruffing squeeze' terminology.

Blocking a key suit is a characteristic of the ruffing squeeze which works here against either defender with the king of hearts and four or more clubs. The tough part is to work out whether the defender who has been squeezed is left with the singleton king of hearts or with ♡K-x. A strong defender in such a situation will often bare the ♡K early and not help you by squirming late in the play.

```
  ♠ K Q J 9 8 7 6                    ♠ A 10 5 4
  ♡ - - -              N             ♡ A 6 5
  ◊ Q 10          W         E        ◊ K 3 2
  ♣ 7 5 4 2            S             ♣ A K 6
```

Dealer South : Neither side vulnerable

WEST	NORTH	EAST	SOUTH
			1♡
4♠	No	6♠	All pass

North leads the 2 of hearts. How would you play?

It is always pleasant to discard a loser on a winner in dummy but it may be vital to choose your moment with care. The bidding marks South with almost all the missing points. You could take the ♡A, discarding a club loser, draw trumps with the ♠K and ♠A and lead a diamond to your ten. If, as expected, South has the ace and jack of diamonds, the ◊10 will win, the ◊Q will force out the ace and you will be able to discard your remaining club loser on dummy's ◊K.

Good as that plan is, you can do better. While it would not be earth-shattering news if the ◊J turned up with North, it is almost 100% certain that the ◊A is with South to justify the opening bid. If so, the slam is safe as long as you ruff the opening lead. You need to keep the ♡A as you do not know at this stage which discard is best.

So, play low from dummy and ruff the heart lead, play ♠K and a spade to the ace, removing all trumps, and then lead the ◊2. If South rises with the ◊A, dummy's ◊K and ♡A eliminate the club losers.

If South plays low on the ◊2, you play the queen which wins. Cross to dummy with a club and discard the ◊A on the ♡A. Concede a club and ruff your last club in dummy. Making six.

The principle of this play (known as 'Morton's Fork') is analogous to a finesse. You force South to choose his play in diamonds before you commit yourself to a discard on the ♡A.

With four seemingly inevitable losers, it is hard to believe that South has any legitimate play in 4♠ on this deal but after West fails to find the diamond lead, the contract cannot be beaten:

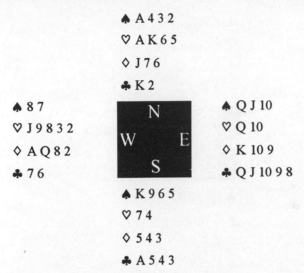

```
                    ♠ A 4 3 2
                    ♡ A K 6 5
                    ◇ J 7 6
                    ♣ K 2
  ♠ 8 7                              ♠ Q J 10
  ♡ J 9 8 3 2          N            ♡ Q 10
  ◇ A Q 8 2        W       E        ◇ K 10 9
  ♣ 7 6                S            ♣ Q J 10 9 8
                    ♠ K 9 6 5
                    ♡ 7 4
                    ◇ 5 4 3
                    ♣ A 5 4 3
```

The secret is not to brood on the four losers. Concentrate on how many winners are available. With four outside winners, South needs six trump tricks. Take the ♣7 lead with the king and cash ♠A, ♠K. After ♡A, ♡K, ♣A, cross-ruff first a club, then a heart, then a club, leaving:

```
                    ♠ - - -
                    ♡ 5
                    ◇ J 7 6
  ♠ - - -                           ♠ Q
  ♡ J                               ♡ - - -
  ◇ A Q 8                           ◇ K 10 9
                    ♠ 9
                    ♡ - - -
                    ◇ 5 4 3
```

The ♡5 is led and South scores the ♠9 for the tenth trick no matter what East does. South is said to have made the ♠9 *en passant*.

The final two deals show declarer overcoming the defenders' seemingly impregnable trump holdings. The first, a 'smother play', sees West's 'sure trump trick' in 6♠ smothered at trick 12.

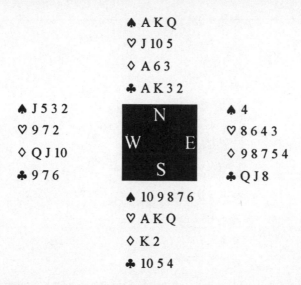

```
                    ♠ A K Q
                    ♥ J 10 5
                    ♦ A 6 3
                    ♣ A K 3 2
    ♠ J 5 3 2          N          ♠ 4
    ♥ 9 7 2          W   E        ♥ 8 6 4 3
    ♦ Q J 10           S          ♦ 9 8 7 5 4
    ♣ 9 7 6                        ♣ Q J 8
                    ♠ 10 9 8 7 6
                    ♥ A K Q
                    ♦ K 2
                    ♣ 10 5 4
```

West leads the ♦Q. You take the ♦K and cash ♠A, ♠K, learning of the vile break. Cash ♥A, ♥K, ♥Q, ♣A, ♣K and ♦A followed by a diamond ruff. Then exit with ♣10 to East's ♣Q, leaving:

```
                    ♠ Q
                    ♦ - - -
                    ♣ 2
    ♠ J 5                          ♠ - - -
    ♦ - - -                        ♦ 9 7
    ♣ - - -                        ♣ - - -
                    ♠ 10 9
                    ♦ - - -
                    ♣ - - -
```

East plays a diamond, South ruffs and whatever West does, declarer wins the last two tricks. You can see how the jack is 'smothered'.

Here the apparent trump trick for the defence in 7♠ vanishes when declarer is able to execute a 'Devil's Coup'.

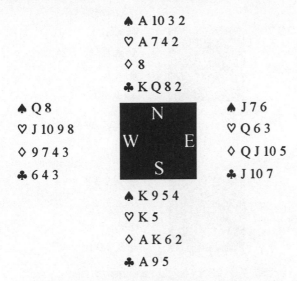

```
                    ♠ A 10 3 2
                    ♡ A 7 4 2
                    ◊ 8
                    ♣ K Q 8 2
♠ Q 8                                    ♠ J 7 6
♡ J 10 9 8          N                    ♡ Q 6 3
◊ 9 7 4 3       W       E                ◊ Q J 10 5
♣ 6 4 3             S                    ♣ J 10 7
                    ♠ K 9 5 4
                    ♡ K 5
                    ◊ A K 6 2
                    ♣ A 9 5
```

Declarer wins the heart lead in hand, cashes three clubs and ◊A, ◊K, discarding dummy's last club. After a diamond ruff, ♡A and a heart ruff, another diamond is ruffed. These are the cards remaining:

```
                    ♠ A 10
                    ♡ 2
        ♠ Q 8                    ♠ J 7 6
        ♡ 10                     ♡ - - -
                    ♠ K 9 5
                    ♡ - - -
```

When the ♡2 is led from dummy, what can East do?

If East ruffs low, South over-ruffs with the ♠9 and the hand is over. If instead East ruffs with the ♠J, South over-ruffs with the ♠K and then finesses the ♠10 to land the grand slam. You can see why it is called a devil's coup, can't you? The defenders had a 'certain' trump trick which has vanished, surely the work of the devil!

THE FINAL QUIZ

(1) *You*

    ♠ A J 10 9 8 7

    ♥ 4

    ♦ 9 7

    ♣ 6 5 3 2

    Dummy

    ♠ K Q

    ♥ A K 7 6 5 2

    ♦ A K

    ♣ A Q J

Contract : 7♠. Lead: ♦Q. North turns up with four trumps. Plan the play.

(2) ♠ K 8 4

    ♥ 9

    ♦ K 10 9 3 2

    ♣ A Q 10 8

    ♠ A 9 3 2

    ♥ A K 5 2

    ♦ A

    ♣ K J 9 6

Contract : 7♣. Lead: ♥Q. Can you foresee any problems?

(3) ♠ - - -

    ♥ K Q 10 5

    ♦ K Q J

    ♣ 10 9 8 5 4 3

    ♠ Q 10 6 2

    ♥ A J 4 3 2

    ♦ A

    ♣ A K J

Contract : 7♥. Lead: ♠A. What is the best line if hearts and clubs both divide 3-1 as expected?

(4) ♠ A 5

    ♥ K 5 3

    ♦ A 6

    ♣ K J 8 7 6 4

    ♠ K Q 4 3 2

    ♥ - - -

    ♦ K 5 4 3 2

    ♣ Q 10 9

Contract : 6♣. Lead: ♣2 to South's ace, South returns the ♣3. The clubs are 2-2. Plan the play.

(5) *You*　　　　　　　　　　　　　*Dummy*

   ♠ A K 6 3　　　　　　　　　　♠ - - -
   ♡ K J 4 2　　　　　　　　　　♡ A Q 5 3
   ♦ 6　　　　　　　　　　　　　♦ A 4 3
   ♣ K Q 10 8　　　　　　　　　　♣ A 7 6 4 3 2

Contract : 7♡. Lead: ♦ K. Plan the play. What could go wrong?

(6) ♠ A K Q 10 9　　　　　　　　　♠ J 8 7
   ♡ Q 8　　　　　　　　　　　　♡ 7 4 3
   ♦ 10 5　　　　　　　　　　　　♦ A 6 4 3
   ♣ A K Q 2　　　　　　　　　　♣ 9 8 4

Contract : 4♠. Lead: ♦ K. Plan the play. Where is the tenth trick?

(7) ♠ 4　　　　　　　　　　　　　♠ A K 7
   ♡ A 8 4 3　　　　　　　　　　♡ 7 6 5
   ♦ K Q J 10 9　　　　　　　　　♦ A 6 2
   ♣ A K Q　　　　　　　　　　　♣ J 10 9 3

Contract : 6♦. Lead: ♠ Q. What is the safest line for twelve tricks?

(8) ♠ A 9 8 7 6 5　　　　　　　　　♠ K 3
   ♡ A K Q　　　　　　　　　　　♡ J 10 4 2
   ♦ - - -　　　　　　　　　　　♦ A 7 6 4
   ♣ A K 7 3　　　　　　　　　　♣ 6 4 2

Contract : 6♠. Lead: ♦ K. There are twelve winners if the trumps are 3-2 but even so, you have some hurdles to surmount. How do you plan to do that?

(9)

You		Dummy
♠ Q 10 9 8 7		♠ A K
♡ A K Q J 10		♡ 7 4 3
◇ 5 3		◇ A K 8 7 6 2
♣ 9		♣ A 3

Contract : 6♡. Lead: ♣K. Plan the play for trumps breaking 3-2 or 4-1 or 5-0.

(10)

♠ 6		♠ A 5 4 3 2
♡ A K Q J 7 6 4 2		♡ 10 9 3
◇ 9		◇ 8 6
♣ 7 4 2		♣ 10 5 3

Contract : 4♡. Lead: ◇K, followed by ◇Q. Will you be able to capitalise on this reprieve?

(11)

♠ A Q 4		♠ 7 3
♡ 8 3		♡ A Q
◇ K Q 7 6 5 4		◇ A J 8 3 2
♣ A K		♣ J 6 4 3

Contract : 6◇. Lead: ♡J. Which path gives you the best chance for ten tricks?

(12)

♠ 9		♠ A K 7 5 3 2
♡ K Q J		♡ 7 4 2
◇ K Q J 5 4 3 2		◇ 6
♣ 7 5		♣ A K 2

Contract : 5◇. Lead: ♡9, two, eight, king. Plan your play.

(13) *You*   *Dummy*

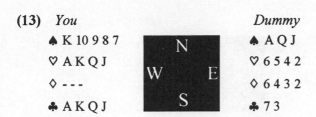

    ♠ K 10 9 8 7   ♠ A Q J
    ♡ A K Q J   ♡ 6 5 4 2
    ◇ - - -   ◇ 6 4 3 2
    ♣ A K Q J   ♣ 7 3

Contract : 7♠. Lead: ◇ K, ruffed. When you play a spade to the ace, South throws a diamond. Can you survive the 5-0 trump break?

(14) ♠ A K 7   ♠ 9 4 3 2
    ♡ K Q J 9 6 5   ♡ A 10 7 3
    ◇ 6   ◇ A 7
    ♣ J 10 4   ♣ 8 5 3

Contract : 4♡. Lead: ◇K. Can you see any hope?

(15) ♠ A K J 6   ♠ Q 10 9
    ♡ A K   ♡ 7 5
    ◇ A Q 8 4 3 2   ◇ 9 7 6 5
    ♣ 7   ♣ A 6 4 2

Contract : 6◇, doubled. At nil vulnerable, South opened 3♡, West doubled for takeout, East bid 4♣ and West jumped to 5◇. East raised this to 6◇, passed back to North who doubled.
Lead: ♡8. Plan the play.

(16) ♠ A 8 7 5 4   ♠ 6 3 2

    ♡ Q 4 3 2   ♡ A 10 7
    ◇ 7   ◇ A K 5 3 2
    ♣ A K 2   ♣ 5 3

Contract : 4♠. Lead: ♣Q. Plan your play.

(17) *You*   *Dummy*

    ♠ A 7 3   ♠ K Q J 10

    ♡ 10 7 3   ♡ A 2

    ◊ A K 6 3 2   ◊ 9 8 5 4

    ♣ A 4   ♣ K Q 3

Contract : 6◊. Lead: ♡K. You win and cash the ◊A, ◊K but South shows out on the second round. How do you continue?

(18) ♠ A K Q 7 6 4   ♠ 9 2

     ♡ 4   ♡ J 6 2

     ◊ 3 2   ◊ A K Q 10 4

     ♣ J 10 4 2   ♣ Q 5 3

Contract : 4♠. Lead: ♡A, followed by ♡K. You ruff and cash ♠A and ♠K but South discards a heart on the second spade. Can you make this contract?

(19) ♠ Q 5   ♠ K J 10 9 8

     ♡ A   ♡ 7 5 3

     ◊ A K Q J 10 9   ◊ 3

     ♣ A K 3 2   ♣ 8 7 6 4

Contract : 6◊ after North opened 3♡. Partner overbid, as usual. *Lead:* ♡K. Is there any chance other than the bare ♠A?

(20) ♠ A 9   ♠ K 2

     ♡ Q 2   ♡ A 8

     ◊ 8 3   ◊ A 10 7 6 4 2

     ♣ A K Q J 6 3 2   ♣ 10 9 7

Contract : 6♣. Lead: ♡9. Is there any hope if South has the ♡K?

(21) *You*   *Dummy*

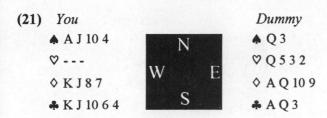

  ♠ A J 10 4   ♠ Q 3

  ♡ - - -   ♡ Q 5 3 2

  ◇ K J 8 7   ◇ A Q 10 9

  ♣ K J 10 6 4   ♣ A Q 3

Contract : 7◇. Lead: ♡A.

(22) ♠ 6 5 4

                                ♠ A K Q J 10

  ♡ A 10 9 7 6 2   ♡ K Q

  ◇ A 10 2   ◇ K Q 8 4

  ♣ 5   ♣ Q 6

Contract : 6♡, after North opened 3♣. Lead: ♣A, followed by ♣K.
You ruff, cash ♡K, ♡Q, but North discards a club on ♡Q. Now?

(23) ♠ K 7 5 3 2

                                ♠ Q J 6 4

  ♡ 9 4   ♡ A 8 6 2

  ◇ K Q 3 2   ◇ J 10

  ♣ A 6   ♣ K Q 7

Contract : 4♠. Lead: ♡K. You take the ace and continue with a
club to the ace and a club to the king. When the ♣Q is played, South
ruffs with the ♠9. What is your plan?

(24) ♠ A K

                              ♠ Q 5 2

  ♡ A K 4   ♡ 9 6 3

  ◇ A K J 10 9 2   ◇ 8 6 5

  ♣ A K   ♣ 8 5 4 3

Contract : 6◇. Lead: ♣Q.

(25) *You*  *Dummy*

♠ A K Q J 10 9	♠ 2
♡ A 4 3 2	♡ K Q J
◊ 9 3	◊ A J
♣ A	♣ 9 8 7 5 4 3 2

Dealer East : Nil vulnerable

WEST	NORTH	EAST	SOUTH
		1♣	5◊
6♠	Double	All pass	

North leads the ♣10. South plays the ◊8.

(26)

♠ 2	♠ A K Q 6 4
♡ Q 10 6	♡ A J
◊ J 5 3	◊ K 2
♣ A K Q 7 4 3	♣ J 10 9 8

Contract : 6♣. Lead: ♡5.

(27)

♠ A K Q 5	♠ J 6 4
♡ A Q	♡ K 8 6 3
◊ 8 5 4	◊ A K 6 3 2
♣ A 8 4 3	♣ 5

Contract : 6♠. Lead: ♠2.

(28)

♠ A K Q 10 9	♠ J 8 7
♡ 7 4 2	♡ 6 5 3
◊ K 7 4 3	◊ A Q 2
♣ 8	♣ A 6 3 2

Contract : 4♠. Lead: ♣Q.

[80]

(29)   *You*   *Dummy*

  ♠ A K Q J   ♠ 5 3
  ♡ A K Q   ♡ 8 6
  ◊ 9   ◊ Q J 8 6 3 2
  ♣ A K J 9 5   ♣ 10 3 2

Contract : 6♣. Lead: ♡J.

(30)   ♠ A K Q J 9 8   ♠ 10 5 3
  ♡ Q 7 4 3   ♡ 2
  ◊ K 8   ◊ A Q 5
  ♣ 2   ♣ A 8 6 5 4 3

Contract : 6♠. Lead: ♠2.

(31)   ♠ 7 5 2   ♠ A 10 6 4
  ♡ K J 9 7 6 2   ♡ A Q 10 3
  ◊ A 6   ◊ 4 2
  ♣ A K   ♣ 7 6 3

Dealer North : Nil vulnerable

WEST	NORTH	EAST	SOUTH
	2♠*	No	No
3♡	No	4♡	All pass

*Weak two, 6-10 points and six spades

Lead: ♠K.

(32)   ♠ A J 9 8 7 6 5 3   ♠ Q 10
  ♡ J 3 2   ♡ K 4
  ◊ A   ◊ J 10 8 7 6
  ♣ 5   ♣ A 7 6 4

Contract : 4♠. Lead: ◊5.

(33)   *You*   *Dummy*

    ♠ 10 7   ♠ A 5 2

    ♡ 8 2   ♡ 9 7 6 5 4 3

    ♦ A J 9 8 7 4 3   ♦ Q 10 2

    ♣ 9 7   ♣ A

Contract : 5♦. *Lead:* ♡A (South playing ♡Q), then ♡K on which
South discards ♠9. North switches to the ♠3.

(34) ♠ A 9 7 5 4   ♠ Q 8 6 3 2

    ♡ A 10 4   ♡ K 9 5 3

    ♦ A 9 6   ♦ K 10 7 4

    ♣ A J   ♣ - - -

Contract : 6♠. *Lead:* ♣K. When you tackle trumps, North has ♠K-J.

(35) ♠ K Q 9 8 7 4 3   ♠ A J 10

    ♡ 7 6   ♡ A 5 4 3 2

    ♦ K 8 4   ♦ 7 3 2

    ♣ 3   ♣ A 9

Contract : 4♠. *Lead:* ♣K.

(36) ♠ 8 2   ♠ 9 6 4 3

    ♡ 6 3   ♡ A K 7

    ♦ A K Q 4   ♦ 7 5 2

    ♣ A K Q J 10   ♣ 8 7 6

Contract : 5♣, after North dealt and opened 1♠. No other North-
South bidding.
Lead: ♠A, ♠K (South discards a heart) and ♠Q (South throws
another heart). Trumps split 3-2.

(37) *You*   *Dummy*

♠ A K Q 6 3 2   ♠ 7 5 4
♡ 8   ♡ A 5 4 3
◇ 9 6 3   ◇ A K 8
♣ A K Q   ♣ 10 5 4

Contract : 6♠. Lead: ♡K.

(38) ♠ J 8   ♠ 9 7 4 2

♡ A J 10 9 7   ♡ K Q 8
◇ A K 5 2   ◇ 7 4
♣ Q J   ♣ K 5 4 2

Contract : 4♡. Lead: ♡2.

(39) ♠ 10 8 7 6   ♠ A Q J 9
♡ 6 5 4 3 2   ♡ A
◇ A K   ◇ 7 4 3
♣ A Q   ♣ 8 6 5 3 2

Contract : 4♠. Lead: ♠2.

(40) ♠ 8 3   ♠ K 10 2
♡ A Q J 9 4 3   ♡ 7 6 2
◇ Q J 6 5   ◇ A K 2
♣ 4   ♣ A K 6 5

Dealer West : N-S vulnerable

WEST	NORTH	EAST	SOUTH
1♡	No	2NT	No
3♡	No	3♠	Double
4♡	No	No	No

Lead: ♠Q. South captures ♠K with ♠A, cashes ♠J (North plays ♠6) and continues with ♠7. What should West play on that?

[83]

(1) After winning the lead, cash the ♠K and overtake the ♠Q with the ♠A. It might seem automatic to complete drawing trumps, but what do you discard from dummy? If hearts break 3-3 or 4-2, you can establish at least two extra winners in hearts and will not need to risk the club finesse. If hearts are 5-1 (or 6-0 with South having the void), you will need to finesse clubs. In order to combine your chances, it is best to abandon trumps for the moment, cross to the ace of hearts and a ruff a low heart from dummy.

If both opponents follow to two rounds of hearts, draw the missing trumps and discard the jack and queen of clubs. Return to dummy with a diamond and cash the king of hearts. If there is still one heart missing, ruff a heart, return to dummy with a diamond and cash two winning hearts to ditch two more club losers.

If either opponent shows out on the second heart, draw the missing trumps and discard two hearts from dummy. Take the club finesse and if it works, cash ♡K, discarding a club, ruff a heart and repeat the club finesse.

(2) You must cash your side suit winners before cross-ruffing. As you can make eight tricks on a cross-ruff, you need only five outside winners. Start with the ace and king of hearts, discarding a spade, followed by the ◇A, ♠A and ♠K. Now proceed with the cross-ruff.

If you tried to cash the king of diamonds, you would probably survive, as a 6-1 break is most unlikely, but there is no need to take the risk. If South did start with a singleton diamond, pray that South does not have the ♣7 when you ruff with the ♣6.

(3) You need precise timing if hearts and clubs are both 3-1. Ruff the ♠A, cash the minor suit aces, return to hand with a low heart to the king, cash the ◇K and ◇Q, discarding both clubs from dummy, ruff the ♣3 with the ♡J and re-enter your hand with a low heart to the queen. If the ♣Q is still out, ruff another club with the ♡A. When a heart to your ten draws the last trump, your hand is high.

(4) You can ruff one heart in dummy and discard one on dummy's extra spade winner but to eliminate the third heart loser, you need to establish an extra winner in spades or diamonds. You will succeed easily if both diamonds and spades break no worse than 4-2, but what if one of these suits breaks 5-1 or 6-0? To cater for a decent break in either suit, it is vital to test the diamonds first.

Suppose you go after the spades first: ♠A, ♠K, ♠Q (pitching a heart) but they prove to be 5-1. Now you can no longer deal with a 4-2 split in diamonds: ◊A, ◊K, ruff a diamond, ruff a heart, ruff a diamond, but there is no way back to dummy to the last diamond.

If you try the diamonds first and they behave, the spades provide an extra entry to dummy. Start with the ace and king of diamonds. If no one has shown out, continue with a diamond ruff, ♠A, ♠K, ♠Q (pitching a heart), ruff the fourth round of diamonds if necessary, ruff a heart loser and discard the other heart on the fifth diamond.

If either opponent shows out on the second diamond, switch to ♠A and a spade to the king. If both follow, cash ♠Q and ruff a spade if a spade is still missing. Ruff a heart to reach dummy's spade winner. As usual, when there is a choice of setting up a long suit or taking a ruff in dummy, play first to set up the long suit. Delay the ruff.

(5) If the clubs are 3-0, they will be blocked after you cash the first three rounds. If the hearts are 4-1 as well, you will fail if you start on trumps at trick 2. The problems can easily be overcome if you spot them in time. Ruff a diamond at trick 2 and continue with ♡K, ♡J and a heart to dummy. Discard the ♣8 on dummy's last heart, cross to ♣K, cash ♠A to discard a diamond and then run the clubs.

(6) You have to lose two hearts and a diamond and so need to do something about a possible club loser. As there are not enough entries to dummy for a dummy reversal, you should plan for a club ruff in dummy. Draw two rounds of trumps with ♠A, ♠K and then cash ♣A, ♣K, ♣Q. You survive if clubs are 3-3, or if the player with three or four trumps has at least four clubs, you can ruff the ♣2 in dummy without hindrance.

(7) You have twelve winners with two spades, one heart, five diamonds and four clubs but the spade lead has removed a vital entry from dummy. To use the extra club winner in dummy, you now need trumps to be 3-2. Best play caters for a 5-1 club break.

Take the ♠A, cash the ♠K and discard ♣Q from hand. Next play the ♠7 and discard ♣K! This play is not exactly intuitive but it is neat. On regaining the lead, cash the ◊K, ◊Q and the ♣A. Then cross to the ◊A and discard three hearts on the ♣J-10-9.

(8) This resembles #7 but looks can deceive. Suppose you take ◊A, discarding ♡Q, cash ♠A, unblock ♡A, ♡K, play a spade to dummy and try to discard losing clubs on ♡J and ♡10. This works if trumps are 3-2 and hearts are 3-3 or if the player with three trumps has four hearts. It fails if the player with three trumps has only two hearts.

Let us try another approach. Suppose you ruff ◊K, cash ♠A and then try ♡A, ♡K, ♡Q. Assuming trumps are 3-2, you are fine if hearts are 3-3. If hearts are 4-2 and the hand with three trumps ruffs the third heart you are still all right. You can draw both missing trumps with a spade to the king and discard two losing clubs on the ◊A and ♡J. This line is clearly superior as the defender with three trumps is more likely to have a doubleton heart than four hearts.

(9) Take ♣A and cash ♡A. If trumps are 5-0, cash ♠A. If ♠J drops, draw trumps, discarding ♠K. If ♠J does not fall, cash ♠K. If ♠J now drops, it is over. If not, play a trump to hand and cash ♠Q. If spades are 3-3, you are home. If not and the player with the trumps has ♠J left, ruff a spade and try ◊A, ◊K. 6♡ is still on if a defender is 4-5-2-2.

If all follow to the ♡A, cash ♡K. If trumps are 3-2, no problems. Draw the last trump and concede a spade if necessary.

If hearts are 4-1, cash the ♠A, draw trumps, discarding the ♠K and continue with ♠Q, ♠10. At worst you lose one spade. If the hearts are 4-1 and spades 5-1, you could fail if you play ♡A, ♡K and then ♠A, ♠K. If a defender ruffs ♠K, you still have another trick to lose.

(10) You can set up an extra spade winner if spades are 4-3 and the hearts 2-1. Ruff the ◊Q but not with the ♡2. Suppose you use the ♡4. Play a spade to the ace and ruff a spade with the ♡A. A lower honour would do but what does it cost to be flamboyant? Play the ♡6 to dummy's ♡10 and ruff another spade high. Use the ♡7 to cross to the ♡9 and ruff the fourth round of spades with a high trump. If all is well, the last spade is a winner and your route to dummy is the carefully preserved ♡2 to dummy's ♡3.

(11) This seems to depend on one of two finesses but paradoxically, if the heart finesse is on, you do not need to take it.

Take the ♡A, draw trumps with the ◊K and if necessary ◊Q. Cash ♣A, ♣K, cross to dummy with a trump and ruff the low club.

If the ♣Q has fallen, re-enter dummy with a trump, discard your losing heart on the ♣J and try the spade finesse for an overtrick.

If the ♣Q does not appear after three rounds of clubs, return to dummy with a trump and ruff the ♣J to create a void in both hands. Now exit with a heart. If North wins, North is end-played and must lead a spade into your tenace, or play a club or heart and allow you to ruff in hand and discard a spade loser from dummy.

If South has the ♡K and leads a spade, you will need the spade finesse. The benefit of taking the ♡A at trick 1 occurs when the ♣Q drops in three rounds. If you take the heart finesse at trick 1 and it loses, you can no longer benefit from the ♣Q falling in three rounds.

(12) Why did South duck the ♡A at trick 1? Has South judged that North has led from a doubleton? If you lead trumps at trick 2, North could take ◊A, lead a heart to South's ace and ruff the heart return.

It may not be good enough to play ♠A and ♠K to discard a heart. If North's trumps are A-10-x, North can still take the ace of diamonds, lead a heart to South's ace and the heart return promotes a trump trick for North. Your best bet is to play a third spade and discard your last heart.

(13) A simple contract becomes a problem when South shows out on the first round of trumps. To survive, cash two hearts and then play on clubs, discarding hearts from dummy.

As long as North cannot ruff on the first two rounds of hearts or clubs, all is well. If North ruffs the third or fourth club, over-ruff and draw trumps. If North does not ruff a club, cross-ruff the rest.

If you fail to cash two rounds of hearts early, North might be able to beat you. If North has a 5-2-4-2 pattern and discards a heart on the third club, you cannot recover and your grand slam is doomed.

(14) Pity you are not in 3NT which would have been easy on the same lead. As the opponents did not start on the clubs, you still have a chance but you will need a subterfuge and a large slice of luck.

Plan (a): Duck ◊K. If North does not produce the club switch, you can discard a spade on the ◊A, play two rounds of trumps, cash ♠A and ♠K, cross to dummy in trumps and ruff a spade. If spades are 3-3, play a trump to dummy and discard a club on dummy's last spade.

Plan (b): Take ◊A and lead a spade to your ♠7. Whoever wins may try to cash a diamond. You ruff, draw trumps and cash ♠A, ♠K. If spades are 3-3, cross to dummy and pitch a club on the last spade.

(15) Surely North has all three trumps to justify the double (a foolish double if it helps you to make the contract). You will need an endplay and to find North with a 4-2-3-4 pattern. Win the lead, cross to ♣A, ruff a club, cross to ♠10 for a second club ruff and overtake ♠J with the ♠Q to complete the elimination of clubs by ruffing.

If North still has a club, cash ◊A and hope trumps are 2-1. If clubs were 4-4, your endplay is alive. Cash ♡K and your remaining spades, ruffing the fourth round in dummy. Now lead a trump and duck it to North who will be end-played if he began with something like: ♠ 8 5 3 2   ♡ 8 4   ◊ K J 10   ♣ K J 9 3

North has had to follow suit to the first ten tricks and has only trumps left at the end. He wins the trump you duck and has to lead a trump back into your A-Q.

(16) Assume trumps are 3-2, otherwise you have no chance. You may be able to create a second winner in hearts but you need not rely on that if the diamonds are 4-3.

Take ♣A, cross to ◊A and ruff a diamond. Now duck a trump. Neither defender can switch to hearts without giving you an extra trick there, so let's suppose they play another club. You win, cash ♠A, ruff ♣2 and cash ◊K. If diamonds have split 4-3, ruff a diamond and enter dummy with ♡A to reach your established diamond. If the diamonds are not 4-3, play the hearts for only one loser (best play is usually low to the queen and if that loses, finesse the ten next time).

(17) After ♡A, play the ◊A and ◊K and when trumps are 3-1, you must aim for two discards on the black suits. To succeed you need the player with the last trump to have at least three spades. Therefore you cannot lose by trying spades first. If they are 3-3, by all means shift to clubs, discarding a heart first on the third club and then another on the thirteenth spade.

The recommended line gains when the defender with the last trump has four spades. You can then discard a heart on the fourth spade before trying the clubs. That could be vital if a defender held specifically a 4-4-3-2 pattern (three diamonds, two clubs), for if you played clubs first, the third round would be ruffed and a heart cashed before you could take a second discard.

(18) The ♠A and ♠K reveal the bad break. Bound to lose a spade, you need to avoid losing more than one club. That means you need three discards on the diamonds before North ruffs in with the ♠J. It follows that if diamonds are 3-3, you will fail, since North can then ruff the fourth diamond and you will have discarded only two clubs.

If 4♠ is to make, you must find North with four diamonds and the odds then favour North holding the ◊J. Cash the ♠Q and then finesse the 10 of diamonds. If that holds, continue with ◊A, ◊K, ◊Q, discarding clubs. If it your lucky day, North will have started with something akin to a 4-3-4-2 pattern and will be unable to ruff diamonds until the fifth round. By then you have only one club left.

(19) This seems next to hopeless since any competent defender will hold off on the first round of spades. Even so, your chances are not so bad. If North began with seven hearts and three or more clubs, you are in business.

After ♡A, you draw trumps, discarding clubs from dummy. Then lead your low spade to dummy's ♠8. If the ace takes this, you are home by overtaking the ♠Q and discarding clubs on the spades. If they duck the first round of spades, ruff a heart, cash the ♣A, ♣K and then play the ♠Q, overtaking with dummy's ♠K. If South began with a 5-2-4-2 or 4-2-5-2 pattern including the ♠A, there is no escape. With only spades left, South can score only the ♠A.

(20) The ♡9 lead makes it almost certain that the ♡K is with South. If you play low from dummy at trick 1 and South wins, it is curtains.

When this deal arose, declarer elected to play South for ♡K and at most one diamond. He took ♡A, drew trumps in two rounds, eliminated spades and cashed ◇A before exiting with a heart. South won ♡K but, with no diamonds left, had to concede a ruff-and-discard, allowing declarer to dispose of his diamond loser. Lucky, but well played!

(21) Your best bet is a dummy reversal, making dummy's four trumps, three heart ruffs in hand, the ♠A and five clubs. Ruff the ace of hearts, play a trump to dummy, ruff a heart, re-enter dummy with a club to the ace and ruff a third heart. Now play a club to dummy's queen and draw trumps, discarding spades from your hand. This line requires the clubs to break 3-2, a better chance than the 50% spade finesse, and diamonds no worse than 4-1.

(22) To nullify South's ♡J-x-x-x, you need to ruff once more to bring yourself down to South's length. Should you play to ruff a spade or a diamond? Suppose you play three rounds of diamonds, South following, and ruff a diamond. If South started with three clubs, as expected, you can no longer succeed. If South is 2-4-4-3 or 1-4-5-3, you are doomed since you will be unable to cash three spades and if South is 3-4-3-3, South can discard a spade on the fourth diamond and ruff the third spade.

After ♡K, ♡Q, play spades next. As long as South has three spades in a 3-4-3-3 or 4-4-2-3 pattern, you can make it. Ruff the fourth round of spades, cash ◇A and play a diamond to dummy. Now play the fifth spade. If South ruffs, it is over. If South discards, pitch your diamond. Now at trick 12 lead a diamond: your ♡A-10 captures South's ♡J-x.

(23) For safety's sake, persevere with your original intention of discarding a heart on the ♣Q. Now, barring a singleton or void diamond with South, nothing can harm you. You may survive if you over-ruff ♠9 but now the risks are greater. Suppose South began with something like: ♠ A 10 9   ♡ 10 7 5 3   ◇ A 8 7 4   ♣ 5 3

After over-ruffing with the ♠K, you lead a trump to dummy's jack. What might happen is that South wins with the ♠A, reaches North's hand with a heart and a fourth round of clubs will promote the ♠10 into an extra winner for the defence. One down.

(24) You have two potential losers, a heart and a diamond. You might make an overtrick by starting with ◇A and ◇K. If the ◇Q is singleton or doubleton, you cash ♠A, ♠K and cross to the ◇8. Discarding your heart loser on the ♠Q gives you thirteen tricks and a feeling of pride, right?

Wrong. At match points, you might play for an overtrick. Otherwise, look for the safest path to twelve tricks. If you start by cashing the top diamonds, you fail if an opponent has ◇Q-x-x or ◇Q-7-4-3.

Best is to win ♣A and lead the ◇9. If the queen takes this, win the return, cash ◇A, ♠A, ♠K, lead a trump to dummy's ◇8 and take your discard on the ♠Q. If the ◇9 holds the trick and one opponent has all four trumps, cash the ♠A, ♠K and lead the ◇J. Now the defender must take the ◇Q or lose it, allowing you to use the ◇8 as entry to dummy and cash the ♠Q with a prayer that it is not ruffed.

If ◇9 holds and both opponents follow, draw trumps and play for thirteen tricks: run all your winners to see whether they manage to keep a heart for the last trick.

(25) Trick 1 marks North with five clubs and six spades, given South's failure to ruff. That means North cannot have three hearts and you must not start by unblocking the ♡K-Q-J. North will ruff. Most likely South has four hearts and nine diamonds. North might have led a singleton diamond and there is some confirmation for North's void in diamonds in the abnormal *ten* of clubs, a suit-preference lead asking for a diamond return if South wins the trick.

Take ♣A, draw six rounds of trumps, discarding clubs from dummy, followed by ♡K, ♡Q, ♡J. If South has let hearts go, overtake ♡J with the ace and your last heart is good. If South has kept four hearts, let ♡J win. Play ♢A and ♢J. South wins but has a heart left. You have been able to use South as a stepping-stone to reach your ♡A.

(26) It is best not to stake everything on the heart finesse. After taking the ♡A, there are two possible routes to success. If the spades are 4-3, you can set up the fifth spade and so discard all your losing diamonds. If the spades are 5-2 or worse, discard two hearts on the ♠K-Q and rely on the ace of diamonds with North.

A 4-3 break in spades at 62% is a better bet than the diamond finesse but you can combine the chances. The key is to delay taking any discard on the spades until you have learnt as much as you can about the spade break. Draw two rounds of trumps, cash the ♠A and ruff a low spade. Play a club to dummy and lead the ♠K.

If both opponents followed to the first two spades and South follows to the ♠K, play for 4-3 spades and discard a diamond. If South shows out on the ♠K, you switch plans, discarding hearts on the ♠K and ♠Q and relying on the ace of diamonds onside.

(27) Assuming spades are no worse than 4-2, you succeed easily if diamonds are 3-2: draw trumps and duck a diamond. It is best not to rely on diamonds, as a 4-1 diamond break (28%) would beat you.

Win the ♠J, cross to ♣A and ruff a club. A heart to the queen allows a second club ruff and a heart to the ace enables you to draw trumps. If nothing bad has happened yet, you have twelve tricks.

(28) There are enough entries in dummy for a dummy reversal as long as trumps are 3-2. Take ♣A and ruff a club. Continue with ♠A and ♠10, overtaking with ♠J. If trumps are 4-1, cash ◊A, ◊Q, ◊K, hoping they are 3-3 or that the hand with four trumps has at least four diamonds as well. If so, you will survive. If trumps are 3-2, ruff another club, return to dummy via ◊A and ruff the last club. A diamond to the queen gives you access to dummy in order to draw the last trump.

(29) As you can do nothing about the diamond loser, turn your attention to avoiding a trump loser. Best play: cash ♠A, ♠K and ruff the third round of spades. Then lead the ♣10, finessing if South plays low. If ♣10 wins, lead dummy's last club and repeat the finesse.

With eight trumps, finessing for the ♣Q is the percentage play. If you cash a top club (to cater for singleton ♣Q with North), then ruff the third spade, dummy has only one trump left and you can finesse only once. You lose a trump trick if South began with ♣Q-x-x-x (when North began with any one of ♣8, ♣7, ♣6 or ♣4 singleton).

The recommended line caters not only for ♣Q singleton, ♣Q-x and ♣Q-x-x with South but also for ♣Q-x-x-x. A low singleton with North is four times as likely as specifically the ♣Q singleton.

(30) Without a trump lead, you could ruff two hearts in dummy. It is still worth exiting with ♡Q at trick 2. If the same defender has ♡A-K and no further trump, you will be able to ruff two hearts in dummy.

If a trump is returned, play to set up clubs. Cash ♣A, ruff a club, ruff a heart, ruff a club. If clubs are 3-3, it is easy. If clubs are 4-2, draw the last trump if trumps were 3-1, play ◊8 to ◊Q, ruff a club, then overtake ◊K with ◊A to cash two clubs for two heart discards.

(31) It would be a blunder to play ♠A. You have ten tricks as long as the ♠A is not ruffed. You can see seven spades and North's opening bid promised a six-card suit. Clearly South is void in spades.

Duck the first spade and also duck the ♠Q continuation. If North plays a third spade, you cannot avoid the ruff, but you will have set up a compensating spade trick in dummy for a diamond discard.

(32) It would be unlucky to fail in 4♠ if you play a heart to the king at trick 2. South would have to have ♡A and return a trump. You rise with ♠A, cross to ♣A and lead a heart towards ♡J. North would have to hold ♡Q and ♠K as well, to remove dummy's last trump.

With each key card wrong, the above line might fail. A foolproof line exists: cross to ♣A and lead ♡4 to ♡J. North wins with ♡Q but cannot lead a spade without losing a trump trick. Either there is no trump loser or you can ruff a heart in dummy to make 4♠. This play has been attributed to the great Italian star, Giorgio Belladonna, but he declined to accept the credit and called it 'journalistic licence'.

(33) Take ♠A, ruff a heart, cross to ♣A and ruff another heart. This sets up two heart winners in dummy. Ruff your club loser with dummy's low trump and lead ♢Q. If South started with ♢K-x, you are home. If South covers, return to dummy with a diamond to the ten and cash hearts. If ♢Q holds and North follows, continue with a winning heart. If South ruffs, over-ruff and re-enter dummy with a diamond to the ten for a spade discard on the last heart. If ♢Q holds and North shows out, continue with a winning heart. South can defeat you by ruffing this, but South may discard. If so, you are home. Pitch the spade loser and revert to the diamond finesse. North in fact held: ♠ J 6 4 3   ♡ A K J 10   ♢ 6   ♣ Q 8 6 3

Would you as North have found the vital spade switch at trick 2?

(34) Declarer, Spanish international Rafael Munoz, ruffed the club in dummy and cashed ♠A. When ♠K did not fall, he needed an endplay and, to remove a club exit, the ♣A was played. What to discard from dummy? Whatever suit is discarded allows the defence to exit in that suit and barring a miracle, there will still be a loser in the other red suit.

Munoz found the answer. He kept both red suits intact by ruffing ♣A! Now he exited with a trump, taken by North who shifted to ♡8. South's ♡Q was taken by ♡A. Next came a finesse of dummy's ♡9 and the 3-3 break in hearts eliminated declarer's loser in diamonds. There was no escape as North had started with:

♠ K J   ♡ J 8 7   ♢ J 8 3   ♣ K Q 10 8 3

(35) You could fail if South gains the lead in hearts, for a diamond switch might give the defence three tricks there. Your best bet is to duck the ♣K lead. North's best move is a trump switch. You win with dummy's ♠10, cash the ♣A and discard a heart. After ♡A and a heart ruff, a spade to the jack allows a second heart ruff. If hearts have split 3-3, return to dummy with a spade and discard two diamonds. If hearts were not 3-3, lead a diamond to your king.

If North fails to switch to a trump at trick 2, dummy has an extra entry and you can establish an extra heart trick even if they are 4-2.

(36) Playing to ruff a diamond in dummy is not best. After ♣A, ♣K reveal that trumps are 3-2, the contract is secure as long as North, already marked with eight black cards, does not hold four diamonds.

Draw the last trump and cash ◇A, ◇K, ◇Q. If diamonds were 3-3, claim. If South had four or more diamonds, it is also over. With four cards left, you have ♡6-3, ◇4, ♣J, and dummy has ♠9, ♡A-K-7.

When you lead ♣J, North must keep a spade, else the ♠9 is high, and so cannot keep three hearts. When North throws a heart, pitch ♠9 from dummy. South has to let go the last diamond or also reduce to two hearts. If South discards a heart, dummy takes the last three tricks.

(37) Take the ♡A and ruff a heart at trick 2. This precaution could be essential if South began with all four trumps. If all follow to the ♠A, you can torture the opponents for a while but the slam is safe.

If North shows out on the ♠A, you still succeed as long as South has at least three clubs and two diamonds. Suppose South began with:

♠ J 10 9 8   ♡ 10 9 2   ◇ Q 10 5   ♣ 9 8 3

After ♡A, heart ruff, ♠A, continue with the ♠K and ♠Q, followed by three rounds of clubs. Cross to dummy with a diamond, ruff a heart, return to dummy and lead dummy's fourth heart. If South has not been able to ruff in yet, you are home. Whether or not South ruffs the fourth heart, you score the last trump and make six spades, one heart, two diamonds and three clubs.

(38) The point is to realise that lack of quick entries to hand will prevent your ruffing two diamonds in dummy. Suppose you start with the ace and king of diamonds followed by a diamond ruff. The opponents can win a black suit exit and lead another trump, leaving you with a diamond to lose as well as the three black losers.

Play the ♣Q at trick 2. If they take the ace and play another trump (best defence), you win, unblock the ♣J, cash the top diamonds, ruff a diamond in dummy and discard a loser on the ♣K. If none of your winners has been ruffed, you are home.

(39) Your best chance is to ruff three hearts in dummy. If you take any finesse and it fails, another round of trumps could spell defeat.

Rise with the ace of spades, cash the ace of hearts, play a diamond to hand and ruff a heart. Another diamond to hand allows another heart ruff. If nothing untoward has taken place, reject the club finesse. A club to the ace and another heart ruff guarantees success with one club, two diamonds, the ace of hearts, three heart ruffs, the ace of trumps so far and two spade tricks still to come in your hand.

(40) If North began with a doubleton spade and K-10-x in hearts, you are doomed whatever you do. If you ruff with the ♡Q or ♡J, North will discard and make two trump tricks later.

If the trump honours are split, you can succeed by ruffing with the ♡9. If this is taken by the king, your worries are over. If the ♡9 loses to the ten, your best bet is to finesse South for the ♡K later.

It is true that if South began with ♡K, ♡K-x or ♡K-x-x, it would work to ruff with the ♡Q or ♡J, but ruffing with an honour exposes you to a different risk. Perhaps North follows to the third spade. The deal arose in the 1997 Bermuda Bowl and North began with:

♠ Q 6 5   ♡ K 10 5   ◊ 9 8   ♣ Q 10 8 3 2

If you ruff with ♡Q or ♡J, North comes to two trump tricks later. In the quarter-final match against the USA, the Chinese declarer ruffed the third spade with the ♡9 and had no problems making 4♡.